ST CUTHBERT'S WAY

ST CUTHBERT'S WAY

Melrose to Lindisfarne

Official Trail Guide

Roger Smith and Ron Shaw

New Revised Edition by Ron Shaw

BIRLINN

First published in 1997 by
The Stationery Office
This second edition published in 2009 by
Birlinn Limited
West Newington House
10 Newington Road
Edinburgh
EH9 1QS

www.birlinn.co.uk

Reprinted with corrections in 2011

ISBN 13: 978 1 84183 131 2

British Library Cataloguing-in-Publication Data
A catalogue record for this book is available from the
British Library

Typeset in Gill Sans and Palatino at Birlinn

Printed and bound by Bell & Bain Ltd., Glasgow

CONTENTS

Foreword to the Revised Edition

St Cuthbert's Way celebrated its 10th Anniversary during summer 2006 with a series of walks and related events.

In the ten years it had been open the route had gained a reputation as one of Britain's most enjoyable long-distance walks, with its rich historic and religious interest and the great variety of terrain encountered along its one hundred kilometre length. Highlights of the route include a high-level crossing of the Cheviot Hills, walking over the Eildon Hills and the Northumberland Fell Sandstone Moors and riverside walking along the Tweed, not to mention the abbeys, churches, castles and prehistoric remains to be seen along the way. The route has also become popular with church groups who walk the Way as a pilgrimage, and a Pilgrim's Guide to the route was published in 2000.

Within a year of the opening of the Way it had received two awards – the first was from the Guild of British Travel Writers which gave it a 'Highly Commended' award for its innovative approach to developing tourism, and the second was from the Eastern Borders Development Association for its outstanding contribution to the economy of the Scottish Borders and North Northumberland. Commemorative plaques for the latter award were handed over to the two people responsible for the creation of the Way and were subsequently affixed to walls at the start and finish of the route – at the Melrose Tourist Information Centre opposite the Abbey, and at Holy Island Post Office.

A cross-border management group has been formed consisting of Scottish Borders Council Ranger Service, Northumberland National Park Ranger Service, Northumberland County Council Countryside Service and the Northumberland Coast AONB Team and – from the private sector – Walking Support, the creator of the

St Cuthbert's Way website, plus one of the originators of the Way.

In 1999, a section of St Cuthbert's Way that links the Southern Upland Way with the Pennine Way became part of the European Long Distance Footpath E2, which runs from Stranraer to Nice.

Over the years there have been a number of minor modifications to the route, and one major rerouting which covers the section between Jedfoot and Cessford. This and the minor changes are included in the text of this revised edition.

All involved in the promotion and upkeep of St Cuthbert's Way trust that you will have an enjoyable experience while walking the Way and hope that this guidebook will help to enhance your pleasure.

Acknowledgements

The St Cuthbert's Way route was developed as a partnership between the Scottish BorderPaths Project and Till Valley Tourism Initiative. Scottish BorderPaths was supported by Scottish Enterprise Borders, Scottish Natural Heritage, Scottish Borders Council and VisitScotland Borders. During its existence the Till Valley Tourism Initiative was supported by Northumberland County Council, Northumberland National Park, Northumbria Tourist Board, the Rural Development Commission and Berwick-upon-Tweed Borough Council. The support of all these organisations is gratefully acknowledged.

We also wish to acknowledge the help of all those who assisted with the development of the route, and in particular all farmers, landowners and land managers along the route, for their co-operation, without which the route would never have been completed.

INTRODUCTION
The Making of the Way

The concept of creating a cross-Border walking route linking places associated with the life of St Cuthbert and thus celebrating in a novel and very interesting manner the life of the 7th century saint came from Ron Shaw, at the time Project Officer with the Till Valley Tourism Initiative, based in Wooler.

In January 1995 Ron contacted Roger Smith, who had been appointed as Walking Development Officer for the Scottish Borders the previous year, and outlined his idea. Roger was immediately enthusiastic. Both men felt that the route would have great appeal to a wide range of walkers.

The next task was to persuade the agencies funding both Roger's and Ron's posts that the idea was worth pursuing. There were eight public agencies involved, and it is to their credit that they were all supportive from the outset. Funds were made available, and a target date of summer 1996 for the opening of the route was set.

This date was extremely ambitious, bearing in mind that most long distance trails in the UK have taken at least five years to set up. However, the proposed route used existing access for much of its length and it was felt that, given the goodwill that the project quickly generated, the target was worth pursuing. Having something to aim for also helps to concentrate the minds of those working on any project!

Over the period of spring and summer 1995, fortunately assisted by generally excellent weather conditions, the route was carefully investigated. It says much for the soundness of the original idea that only short sections were altered from the line drawn on maps early in the year. Once the line to be taken had been agreed, detailed surveying was carried out to establish exactly how much work was needed on the ground, both in terms of infrastructure such as stiles and gates, and also where waymarking would be needed to keep walkers heading the right way. Countryside ranger services on both sides of the Border were involved in this work and offered invaluable advice. The symbol of St Cuthbert's Cross was agreed as the waymark for the route, and from the outset it was accepted that the route would be fully waymarked in both directions.

In terms of access, agreements had to be negotiated with landowners and managers for several sections on the Scottish side where public paths had not previously existed. These included principally the section from Crailinghall to Cessford (now no longer part of the route) and the section from the Kale Water to Crooked-shaws, between Morebattle and Yetholm. In addition, short sections of permissive path were agreed on the English side.

All known landowners, managers and farmers were contacted and provided with details of the route across their land, and exact locations for waymark posts, stiles and other structures on the ground. In all over 40 land-owners and farmers were involved, and the task of getting the agreements finalised went on through the winter of 1995-96 and into the spring of 1996.

The only major piece of work needed was a new foot-bridge over the Kale Water east of Morebattle, replacing an old bridge which was unsafe. The splendid new bridge spans the water in a single stride of 14 metres and was constructed by Colin Robertson of Charlesfield in July 1996, just in time for the opening of the route.

There was a great deal of other work to be done in terms of new stiles, gates and waymark posts. On the Scottish side the majority of this work was carried out by one of Scottish Enterprise Borders' Environment Action teams. These teams were basically long-term unemployed people with a professional supervisor. They did a great job and came to regard the walk as 'their' route.

The Kale Water to Crookedshaws section was prob-ably the most difficult, with material having to be carried up the hill each day before work could start. The ranger services on both sides of the Border also carried out considerable amounts of work, as did volunteer groups in Northumberland. One of these was a group of students from the Countryside Skills Course at Kirkley

Hall College, who undertook path clearance and bridge and stile building which gave them valuable practical experience in the field.

At times it seemed that the work would never be completed for the opening date, but herculean efforts over the closing weeks got everything ready, and the Way was inaugurated at two equally pleasant but distinctively different ceremonies in late July 1996. At the magnificent ruin of Melrose Abbey, St Cuthbert himself made a reappearance after 1300 years to give the new walk his blessing, hoping that it would become a modern pilgrimage in his memory. Three days later in Wooler, a large group of people walked part of the route to 'first foot' it in splendid style.

The creation of St Cuthbert's Way is a happy story and a splendid example of co-operation across a Border which in the past saw more than its fair share of strife. Great credit attaches to everyone involved, and particular thanks are due to all those over whose land the route passes. It is up to all of us walking the route to ensure that it becomes an accepted part of life, complementing the agricultural and forestry operations which take place all year round and not disrupting them.

One of the reasons for creating the route was to provide economic benefit for the communities through which it passes and others close to the route. There is no doubt that this has happened, and as the route continues to become better known, this benefit should increase. The Way has been carefully designed to be manageable by a wide range of walkers. It is not just for the macho backpacker but can be tackled by anyone with reasonable fitness.

The concept of 'trail design' is not widely known in Britain, but models from as far away as South Africa have been studied in the preparation of St Cuthbert's Way, and lessons learned in other countries applied wherever appropriate. The aim throughout has been to give the walker the best possible experience, and to provide the facilities walkers need at regular intervals.

The least satisfactory section is that between Cessford and Morebattle, where for the time being the route has to follow roads. Even here the walking is by no means unpleasant, but we hope that in future years, at least some of this section can be moved off the road. We were keen

to take the route past Cessford Castle, a superb example
of a Border keep.

There is plenty of accommodation along the Way, from
campsites and youth hostels to guest houses and hotels.
Further practical details about walking St Cuthbert's Way
are in the next section. Putting the route together was ex-
hausting, exhilarating and tremendously enjoyable, and
with its range of landscapes and great historical interest
it should continue provide a walking experience of high
quality for many years to come.

We are sure that St Cuthbert, if he were to walk the
route today, would indeed give it his blessing.

Photo Credits

All photographs are by Ron Shaw except for images on
the following pages: those on pp. 73 and 86 are by Tony
Derbyshire, Northumberland County Council; p. 54,
John Steele, Northumberland National Park; p. 66, Phil
Bradley, Northumberland County Council; pp. 79 and 80,
© Gavin Duthie, Northumberland Coast AONB.

WALKING THE WAY

Equipment and Safety

The route of St Cuthbert's Way includes low level stretches along riverside paths and in the Northumberland coastal area as well as more strenuous stretches across the Eildon Hills and through the Cheviot Hills between Morebattle and Wooler. Although the route is waymarked throughout with the St Cuthbert's Cross symbol, a reasonable level of fitness and navigational skill is needed, especially in poor weather conditions. Suitable footwear, warm and waterproof clothing, food and drink, maps and compass are all necessities.

NB: check at the Tourist Information Centre in Wooler for safe crossing times to Holy Island (Lindisfarne). Times are shown on the door when the office is closed. Alternatively, phone the Tourist Information Centre in Berwick (01289 330733) or visit the County Council website (www.northumberland.gov.uk) for advance details of tide tables.

Access and Maps

Within Scotland St Cuthbert's Way follows proven rights of way or routes where access has been agreed with landowners as well as public roads, and within England it follows public footpaths, bridleways and byways, permissive paths agreed with landowners and public roads.

Ordnance Survey (OS) Explorer maps covering the full route are Nos 338 Galashiels, Selkirk and Melrose, OL16 The Cheviot Hills and 340 Holy Island and Bamburgh at a scale of 1:25,000. The route is marked on these maps.

Waymarking

The route is waymarked throughout with the St Cuthbert's Cross symbol. Where this symbol appears on its own it indicates that the route goes straight on, unless it is accompanied by a separate direction turning arrow. Where the symbol appears with an arrow, it indicates that the route turns. Some 'straight on' points where the route ahead is unclear are marked with the symbol and a straight on arrow. Significant points are also marked with tall fingerposts.

Routes through villages and at some road junctions in Scotland are marked by metal signs with the St Cuthbert's Cross symbol. In Northumberland standard tourism white on brown signs are used in these situations.

The waymarking has been carefully prepared to show all significant points and turns on the route, and to enable walkers to follow the route in either direction. If you experience any difficulty or feel the waymarking could be improved, please let us know.

Car parking

There are recognised car parks or parking areas at the following places along the route:

Melrose – several pay and display or free car parks

Bowden – park considerately in the village

Newtown St Boswells – large pay and display park by the auction mart

St Boswells – pay and display park next to public toilets and bus stance (please do *not* use the golf club car park)

Maxton – car park at church (reserved for churchgoers' use on Sunday mornings)

Harestanes – large free car park at visitor centre

Jedfoot – room for two cars at start of Dere Street section

Cessford – park considerately in the village

Morebattle – park considerately in the village

Town Yetholm/Kirk Yetholm – park considerately in the villages

Halterburn Road – on the large grass area by the cattle grid

Hethpool – College Valley car park

Wooler Common – Forest Enterprise car park

Wooler – several pay and display or free car parks in the town

East/West Horton – park considerately in the village

St Cuthbert's Cave – National Trust car park at Holburn Grange

Fenwick – park considerately on the road leading into the village from the south

Beal – Causeway free car park

Holy Island – Chare Ends pay and display car park

Please do not park elsewhere along the route, as to do so will cause inconvenience and possible difficulty for residents, or disruption to farm or estate operations. Your co-operation in this matter is greatly appreciated. In particular, please be very careful not to block farm access roads or gateways.

Accommodation and Services

Accommodation lists for their respective areas are issued by Visit Scotland Borders Information Service – www.visitscottishborders.com (0870 608 0404) and Northumberland Tourism – www.visitnorthumberland.com (01670 794 520). Tourist Information Centres on or near the route will be found at Melrose, Jedburgh, Wooler and Berwick Upon Tweed. These centres can provide information and assistance on accommodation, travel, visitor attractions and activities.

Please note that on the English section under no circumstances should you camp anywhere along the route, other than on established campsites, without first getting the express permission of the landowner.

In Scotland wild camping is permissible under the Scottish Outdoor Access Code. This type of camping is lightweight, done in small numbers and only for two or three nights in any one place. You can camp in this way wherever access rights apply but help to avoid causing problems for local people and land managers by not camping in enclosed fields of crops or farm animals and by keeping well away from buildings, roads or historic structures. Take extra care to avoid disturbing deer stalking or grouse shooting. If you wish to camp close to a house or building, seek the owner's permission.

Further information can be found at:
www.outdooraccess-scotland.com

Other useful websites are:

www.visitscottishborders.com/What to See/Walking/
Routes/StCuthbertsWay

www.stcuthbertsway.net

www.northumberland-national-park.org.uk

www.northumberland.gov.uk

www.northumberlandcoastaonb.org

For information and timetables of bus services both sides of the Border contact www.traveline.org.uk or phone 0871 200 2233.

The Countryside Code in England

Walkers are reminded to follow the Countryside Code:

- Be safe – plan ahead and follow any signs
- Leave gates and property as you find them
- Protect plants and animals and take your litter home
- Keep dogs under close control
- Consider other people

The Scottish Outdoor Access Code

Know the Code before you go…
Enjoy Scotland's outdoors – responsibly!
Everyone has the right to be on most land and inland water for recreation, education and for going from place to place provided they act responsibly. These access rights and responsibilities are explained in the Scottish Outdoor Access Code. The key points are:

When you are in the outdoors:

- Take responsibility for your own actions and act safely
- Respect people's privacy and peace of mind
- Help land managers and others to work safely and effectively

- Care for your environment and take your litter home
- Keep dogs under proper control
- Take extra care if you are organising an event or running a business

Find out more by visiting: www.outdooraccess-scotland.com.

Take only photographs, leave only footprints

Livestock

The new Scottish Outdoor Access Code gives strict advice on access to the countryside with a dog. Dogs are a great cause of concern for farmers, especially during lambing time (March-May) and when cows have young calves with them (mainly in the spring and autumn, although some farms do calf all year round).

Dogs should be kept on a lead or under very close control at all times, especially during the ground nesting season for birds (April-July). Cattle and sheep, particularly those with young, should not be approached.

Dogs should not be taken into fields with cattle when they have young, as the cows see the dog as a threat and may try to attack it; nor should they be taken into fields containing sheep with young lambs. At the most sensitive times of year such as lambing, calving and during the ground nesting season for birds, it is recommended that you leave your dog at home. Without a dog, if you walk quietly through livestock areas, you should experience few if any problems.

Note

The St Cuthbert's Way route has been developed primarily as a footpath. Apart from those sections of the route in England which are established bridleways, the route is not intended for use by either cyclists or equestrians. In some areas landowners have expressly asked that cyclists and equestrians should not be permitted on the route: please comply with this request where indicated.

In Scotland, the Scottish Outdoor Access Code gives a right of responsible access for walking, cycling and horse riding. However, there are sections of St Cuthbert's Way which may be unsuitable for use by cyclists and horses.

Comments on the route are welcome and can be sent to either of the addresses given under 'Accommodation and Services'. Comments regarding infrastructure, missing or damaged stiles, waymarks etc can also be sent to the Countryside Access Team, Scottish Borders Council, Newtown St Boswells, Melrose, TD6 0SA (01835 826509) for the Scottish section of the route, or to the Countryside Service, Northumberland County Council, County Hall, Morpeth, NE61 2EF (01670 533 000) for the English section.

St Cuthbert

The life and progress of St Cuthbert has provided the inspiration for this route to be developed. Contemporary accounts indicate that St Cuthbert started his ministry at Old Melrose (see page 2) in about 650AD. Before that, the picture is less clear. Some claim that he was born and raised in Lauderdale, on the Scottish side of the Border; others that his birthplace was in Northumberland.

All are agreed that Cuthbert received a very strong call to the ministry when aged about 16. He travelled to Melrose, where his saintliness was recognised by St Boisil, who was the prior at the monastery, and by Eata, the abbot of Melrose. Cuthbert was admitted and joined the way of life of the brothers, in prayer, study and work outside in the fields.

His qualities of leadership were soon apparent, and Eata asked Cuthbert to accompany him to Ripon in North Yorkshire, where a new monastery was to be established. Cuthbert was not entirely happy to leave Melrose, but saw where his duty lay. There were problems at Ripon as Bishop Wilfrid, a strong supporter of the Roman church, had many followers in the area. Wilfrid resented the new foundation and used his influence with King Alhfrith to have the monastery closed and the brothers expelled.

Cuthbert returned to Melrose, and found he was afflicted with the 'yellow plague' which swept across Europe at this time, killing up to half the population. He declined near to death, but was saved by the power of prayer, an experience he never forgot. Then Boisil, his friend and teacher, died of the same plague, and Cuthbert became prior at Melrose. He travelled widely, visited people in the remoter parts of the area, and must have grown to know the Border country very well. Often he took shelter in the hills.

Cuthbert's reputation grew, and he became known as 'the Fire in the North'. Above all he loved the sea and the coastal landscape and islands, and he spent some time at the monastery of St Ebba at Coldingham (St Abbs is

named after her). Ebba was a princess of royal blood
and presided over a monastery with both brothers and
sisters living and working there. Cuthbert spent much
of his time by the sea, praying, and it is said that the sea
creatures such as seals and otters came to him, unafraid,
and received his blessing.

At this time he also made a journey to the north of
Scotland to spread the Christian word, but his destiny lay
further south, and he followed in the footsteps of St Aidan
to the holy island of Lindisfarne to be prior. While here,
he became even more famous for his saintliness and his
healing powers. Cuthbert's life grew ever busier; he had
less and less time for the reflection and prayer that were
so important to him, and he grew increasingly aware of
a need within himself for solitude.

He moved first onto St Cuthbert's Isle, just off Holy
Island (also called Hobthrush). But even this was too near
the monastery, and Cuthbert finally obtained permission
from Eata to go to Inner Farne, where he lived as a hermit
in a small beehive-shaped enclosure. It is said that he
went to Farne 'as a soldier of Christ to do battle with the
powers of darkness'. Again he studied the natural world,
the elements and the sea creatures. Among his favour-
ites were the eider ducks, which came to him to be held.
They began to be called 'Cuthbert's ducks', affectionately
shortened to 'Cuddy ducks', a name by which they are
still known in the area today.

His period of solitude did not last. A great synod
was convened by King Egfrith, attended by Archbishop
Theodore from Canterbury, at which Cuthbert was
unanimously elected as a Bishop of the church. Cuthbert
was at first unwilling to take on what he saw as an extra
burden on him, and he declined to answer when called.
Eventually Bishop Trumwine and other clergy made the
hazardous journey to Inner Farne to plead with Cuthbert.
He recognised the call came from God, and agreed to the
Bishopric. He travelled to Twyford, on the mainland, to
meet the king and the Archbishop. Most historians believe
that 'Twyford on the Aln', as Bede described it, was on
the site of the village of present-day Alnmouth.

The suggestion was that Cuthbert should become
Bishop of Hexham, but he was unhappy with this idea
as it was so far from the sea. He travelled back to Melrose

to discuss matters with his old friend Eata, and a happy solution was found. Eata would assume the Bishopric of Hexham and Cuthbert would become Bishop of Lindisfarne.

His consecration took place at York in the spring, and for several years he travelled widely, as he had when a young man, preaching the Gospel and healing the sick.

Eventually, feeling his life on earth was due to end, he returned to Inner Farne, and died there. His body was taken back to Lindisfarne for burial. Eleven years later his coffin was opened, and his body was found to be perfectly preserved, which led to his canonisation and the foundation of the cult of St Cuthbert. In the following century the Community of St Cuthbert was responsible for the Lindisfarne Gospels, perhaps the greatest work of art of the Anglo-Saxon period.

In 875AD, following a number of Viking raids, the Community left the island with the saint's relics for an eight-year journey around the north of England and the west of Scotland. The relics were said to have rested in the spot now known as St Cuthbert's Cave on the first night off the island. The route of St Cuthbert's Way thus links a number of places associated with his story. Some of the numerous books about the saint can be purchased at the village church or at shops on Holy Island.

What can we find in Cuthbert's life that is relevant to us today? His faith was without question, but it was a faith based on a deep knowledge and understanding of the natural world. He was never afraid of phenomena such as storms or winter snows, seeing them as a part of the seasonal round. He loved all wild creatures and befriended them.

It is clear from accounts of his life that Cuthbert found great solace and true refreshment in walking. Travelling at a natural pace on foot allows time for contemplation, and for the cares and worries that surround us daily to be forgotten, for a while at least. Walking St Cuthbert's Way can thus be enjoyed as a modern pilgrimage. There is still plenty of wildlife, and you may well experience variations of weather that would test a saint!

MELROSE

The town of Melrose is a pleasant place in which to spend some time. The compact town centre features a number of interesting shops where you can buy souvenirs, and there is an excellent selection of cafes, restaurants and hotels for a meal or a drink.

Visitor attractions include, of course, the great abbey – see below – and the National Trust for Scotland's Priorwood and Harmony Gardens. The Ormiston Institute in Market Square includes an exhibition on Roman times and Trimontium.

As with other Border towns, Melrose is passionate about its rugby. Melrose was the place where the exciting sport of Rugby Sevens originated, and the Melrose Sevens, held each April, provides a magnificent day's sport, with invited teams from England and often much further afield, even Australia on occasions. The rugby ground is at Greenyards, about 800 metres from the start of the walk.

Melrose Abbey

One of the four great Border Abbeys, Melrose was founded in 1136 by King David I for Cistercian monks who had come here from Rievaulx in North Yorkshire. They were famed for their farming and horticultural skills, and the Abbey owned large areas of land in the Borders. When complete, the Abbey covered a very much larger area than it does today, but even now the remaining ruin is extremely impressive in size and scale.

By the end of the 14th century, much of the original building had been destroyed during the frequent English raids, and most of what you see today is 15th or 16th century. The reconstructed church represents the high point of Scottish architecture of the time. A feature of the Abbey is the wonderful range of carvings, many showing more than a touch of humour. You can find a cook with ladle,

Opposite: a window in Melrose Abbey.

a fat monk and even a pig playing the pipes! Beneath the chancel is said to lie the heart of Robert the Bruce, and a little to the south is the tombstone of King Alexander II, who died on the island of Kerrera near Oban in 1249.

By the beginning of the 19th century the Abbey, long abandoned, had fallen into decay, but in 1822 the then Duke of Buccleuch began a programme of restoration, and later gifted the Abbey to the nation. Today it is cared for by Historic Scotland, and is open to visitors all year round.

Old Melrose

It is believed that the site of the monastery where St Cuthbert lived and worked as a young man was Old Melrose,

Melrose Abbey and the Eildons.

which is on a bend of the Tweed 4km east of the present town. The original name seems to have been Maelros or Malrhos, which would mean 'bare promontory'. Some maps show the legend 'Site of St Cuthbert's Chapel' at this point. A little south of here is a place called Monksford, indicating a possible crossing place on the river. When King David I granted land at Little Fordell for the abbey foundation, the monks took the name Melrose with them to their new home.

River Tweed

The Tweed is one of the largest rivers in Britain. It runs for approximately 160km (100 miles) from its source high in the Tweedsmuir Hills near Moffat to Berwick-upon-Tweed, where it empties into the North Sea. From Carham to near Berwick the river forms the border between England and Scotland. Because of its natural importance both in terms of biology and hydrology, the complete river channel has been designated a Site of Special Scientific Interest and a Special Area of Conservation.

The course of the Tweed has changed much over the centuries, and near Newstead the old channel of the river is beautifully marked. What was formerly a deep pool and most perilous eddy, or whirlpool, across which Claverhouse is said to have been ferried at the time of the first Jacobite Rising in the late 17th century, is now a meadow, but still continues to be called the Eddy.

The first part of St Cuthbert's Way, as far as Maxton, is never far from the Tweed, and for part of the way actually follows the river bank along a particularly beautiful section.

Newstead

Newstead is an attractive and peaceful little village, at one time the lodging-place for those master craftsmen who put their skill into the building of Melrose Abbey. Located by the site of a bridge which was used by Roman armies, Newstead is able to boast a history stretching back for close on 2,000 years. At one time it was noted for the number of its houses with sundials. Most of these have vanished over time.

The Eildon Hills

It is very tempting to think of the Eildon Hills as long-dead volcanoes, but in fact only Little Hill, located between Mid and Wester Hills, and Chiefswood Quarry by Melrose, are truly volcanic in origin. The three main hills are the result of activity below the earth's crust some 350 million years ago – now exposed after millions of years of weathering. The technical name for such an intrusion is a 'composite laccolith'. Thus are discredited those tales of Michael Scot, famous wizard of the 13th century, for they claim that he it was who clove the head of Eildon into three. Still, it's a nice story!

The Eildons are composed mainly of fairly acid rocks which in turn have weathered to produce acidic soils. As a result, much of the area is covered with an acid heath vegetation which includes heather moor, blaeberry (mainly on North Hill), wavy hair grass and rock screes. Because Little Hill is made of more basic rock, it supports a different vegetation, including many herbs. Lower down the slopes you find the older sedimentary rocks of the Borders, which are more fertile than the volcanic rocks and can thus support agriculture, both livestock and arable, and forestry (and indeed the golf course, which is clearly seen from the col).

Tales of the Eildons are slow to die. Even now there are many who believe that King Arthur lies deep within these hills, having died in a great battle but a few miles away. It is said that he is surrounded by an army of sleeping warriors, ready to leap up to the defence of their country if required. Their sleep must be profound indeed, for they have missed many opportunities in the past 1500 years...

On a clear day, the view from the top of the Eildons is stunning. To the north lie the Lammermuir and Moorfoot Hills, to the west the hills of Upper Tweeddale, the highest in the Borders, and southward stretch the Cheviots, forming the border with England. The line of the Roman Dere Street, now partly followed by the A68, is quite clear, and the site of Trimontium can be seen down beside the Tweed. On the summit of Mid Hill is a viewpoint indicator dedicated to Sir Walter Scott, whose favourite view was from Bemersyde Hill, looking west towards the Eildons.

The Eildon Hills from near Maxton.

Two thousand years ago, the central area of the Tweed Valley was inhabited by the Votadini tribe. Their fort or 'oppidum' on the summit of North Eildon was defended by three stone ramparts, enclosing an area of 20 acres; the remains of these ramparts can be clearly picked out from the lower slopes of the hill, but are best seen from the top of Mid Hill.

Within the walls of the fort were 296 round houses, the dwellings of the Chief and his warrior aristocracy, who were supported by tribute levied on the peasant farmers of the tribe. Life was however far from idyllic, as the Votadini were often in conflict with the Selgovae, who ruled the area to the west. Another major centre for the Votadini will be passed later in the walk at Yeavering Bell (page 54). The name Eildon first appears in 1128 as Aeldonam, which may mean 'fire hill', possible referring either to the fires from the huts on the summit area, or to the fact that beacons were lit to warn of approaching danger.

In 80AD the Votadini were overtaken by disaster. Julius Agricola, the Roman Governor of the British Province, massed his legions for the final conquest of the British Isles. With an overwhelming force of battle-hardened troops he struck north across the Cheviot Hills. They constructed many campsites, each protected by a ditch and palisaded ramparts, within which were pitched disciplined rows of leather tents. The ramparts of one of the great camps can still be seen at Pennymuir on Dere Street, south-east of Jedburgh.

The fort on North Eildon was quickly overcome. The following year a permanent fort, Trimontium, was built just south of the minor road (now declassified) which runs from Newstead to Leaderfoot. Nothing can be seen above ground today except the modern monument marking the spot, but extensive excavations have revealed that over a period of 100 years and six distinct periods of occupation the Romans built a total of four forts on the site, showing its pivotal position in the network of roads and forts that controlled southern Scotland. On the summit of North Eildon you can still make out the low circular rampart within which stood the Roman signal platform.

The line of Dere Street, the Roman road leading to Trimontium from the south, can be clearly picked out from the Eildon summits. The road would have continued, crossing the Tweed by a bridge, heading west of north up Lauderdale. Many wonderful objects have been recovered from Trimontium. Some can be seen in the small collection in Melrose, though the most spectacular finds are reserved for the Museum of Scotland in Edinburgh.

Trimontium was abandoned in 180AD after a confederation of northern Scottish tribes overran the Antonine Wall, slaying a Legionary Legate at the head of his troops. Although victory was gained in 184AD, the fort was never rebuilt and the Romans relied instead on long-range patrols and subsidies paid to local tribes to keep the peace north of Hadrian's Wall.

Wildlife

On the poor acid soils on the higher slopes grow heather, mostly ling and some bell heather, and blaeberry. Here live a few pairs of red grouse which are dependent on heather for food. These birds are difficult to see but can often be located by their characteristic 'goback, goback' call. Here too can be found the common small brown meadow pipit feeding on insects or nesting in the heather, and above the hills kestrels are often seen hunting for small mammals. On the richer soils of Little Hill, a larger

Dere Street at Jedfoot.

variety of flowering plants can be found, including birds-foot trefoil, wild thyme and mountain pansy.

On the lower slopes gorse has invaded the hillsides. Although a nuisance to walkers, it provides an excellent habitat for many small birds such as linnet, dunnock, wren and willow warbler, as well as providing cover for rabbits and foxes. The gorse has also allowed trees to recolonise the hills by providing protection from grazing sheep and cattle.

Among the hedgerows on the farmland and along the edges of woodland yellowhammer, chaffinch and sparrowhawk can all be seen, and in the fields roe deer may occasionally be observed feeding.

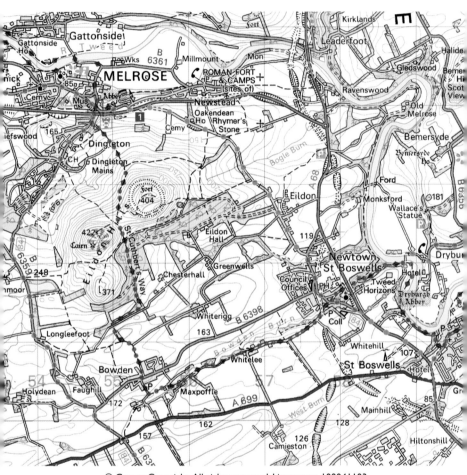

I
MELROSE TO ST BOSWELLS

SUMMARY

Distance: 12km (7.5 miles).

Height Range: 80-320m.

Accommodation: Hotels and B&Bs in Melrose, Bowden, Newtown St Boswells and St Boswells. Youth hostel and campsite in Melrose.

Food and Drink: Available in Melrose, Newtown St Boswells and St Boswells.

Public Transport: Borders Rail Link bus from Berwick to Melrose. Regular bus services to Melrose and St Boswells from Edinburgh, Kelso and Jedburgh.

Terrain Summary: Steep climb from Melrose to the saddle between the Eildon Hills, then a pleasant woodland walk down to Bowden. Burn and riverside walking to St Boswells. A varied first day's walk.

The walk starts at Melrose Abbey, a 12th century Cistercian foundation which is nowadays a magnificent ruin. It is owned by Historic Scotland and is open all year. From the Abbey, walk south to the Square. Cross over and go up the Dingleton Road, under the bypass road bridge. About 150m after the bypass, turn left following the waymarks (which also show the Eildon Walk) between houses. Climb a long flight of steps and then continue steeply uphill along fenced paths through two gates to reach steps and a wicket gate which leads onto the open hill. Continue following the signs half right, climbing steadily on a clear path to the saddle between the two main Eildons. Climb either or both if you wish. Both command magnificent panoramic views of the Borders, and Mid Eildon (on your right) has a view indicator at the summit. Below you to the north-west is Melrose Golf Course on its hilly site, while further away towards Galashiels is the Borders General Hospital.

Eildon Woods.

Continue over the saddle, heading just left of a small quarry to join a wide track. Enter the woods, which are part of an extensive area managed by Buccleuch Estates, at a gate displaying a Walkers Welcome sign, and continue along the track. Keep right at a track junction. The woods include fine mature trees, both broadleaved and conifer, which provide the habitat for a good range of birds and small mammals.

Grey squirrels are common, but the native red variety are much rarer. The woods are also home to foxes and badgers, and roe deer may be seen. Birds include many different finches, jays, wood-pigeons and occasional buzzards.

At a bend in the track carry straight on to the wood edge, with the farm of Chesterhall visible to the left. Head downhill on a winding path. Continue to follow the markers to the foot of the wood at its left-hand side. Turn right and walk inside the edge of the wood to its far end. Turn left through a gate across a red track and continue with the clear path, climbing steps through a small plantation to cross the common and enter Bowden village.

Bowden is an attractive and quiet small village. It has always been closely associated with agriculture, and also, especially in the 18th century, with weaving. It is now a Conservation Area. At its centre is the former school, which was restored by the National Trust for Scotland some years ago. On its front gable is a plaque indicating that the minister at the time of opening in 1831 was the Reverend Thomas Jolly!

The history of Bowden dates back to the 12th century, when it is mentioned in the extant copy of the Foundation Charter of Kelso Abbey. An unfortunate clerical error in the first sentence, 'Bothendene' for 'Bothildene', gave rise to an attractive but spurious legend that Bowden Kirk was dedicated to an obscure Celtic monk called Bothen, said to have been a contemporary of St Cuthbert. The consistent spelling of the name in the records of Kelso Abbey – Bothildene – means 'the valley with a building'. In the development of Middle Scots, this changed over the centuries to Boulden and then to Bowden. Between 30 and 80 husbandmen from the village were obliged to give help to the Abbey at ploughing, sheep-shearing and harvest. Each had to provide the monks with a quantity of ale and a large chicken every Christmas.

The octagonal building under the tree is a former well, and nearby is the old Mercat Cross, which has been adapted for use as a war memorial. Notable people associated with Bowden include Thomas Aird, who was born here in 1802 in the house now called Aird Cottage. He became a well-known writer and poet, and was editor of the *Dumfries Herald* for 28 years.

Another notable Bowden man was Sir Lauder Brunton. Born here in 1844, he went on to make many discoveries in the field of medicine, including the use of amyl nitrate to treat angina and the benefits of using digitalis as a stimulant for heart disease. He died in London in 1916 and is commemorated in Bowden Kirk. Not far from Bowden is Holydean, an estate which was at one time owned by the Kers of Cessford, whose castle you will pass later in the walk.

From the well, turn right and then first left, signposted for Bowden Kirk. Where the lane swings right, go left on a path (or go right if you wish to visit the Kirk, then come back to this point). Bowden Kirk is a lovely old building well worth the short diversion. There has been a church on this site since the 12th century. Much of the present building is at least 300 years old, and inside is a 17th century Laird's Loft bearing the shield and crest of the Kers. The kirkyard contains many interesting gravestones and the fine entrance gates date from 1890.

Bowden village.

Close by is Maxpoffle House. The rather curious-looking name, first given as 'Makispofil' in the 13th century, is said to mean 'a portion of land belonging to Maccus or Magnus'. The same personal name is at the root of Maxton, met a few miles further on, so perhaps he was a major landowner in the area.

Keep on the path, staying on the left side of the attractive little Bowden Burn as far as possible until you have to cross it by a small bridge. On the far side go up the slope, and at the top, go left. Continue on a very clear path to the road at Whitelee. There are often horses in this section. Just as you meet the road, if you look down to your left you will see a substantial stone bridge in the field, with a track crossing it. The size of the bridge indicates that this was an old road to Bowden, now long disused. Walk ahead along the road from Whitelee into Newtown St Boswells.

Just before **Newtown**, you pass underneath a disused railway line. A little south of here there was formerly a very important junction, where the track divided, one branch heading south for Hawick, the other swinging west towards Kelso. Although Kelso is 16km (10 miles) away, the junction was still called Kelso Junction.

The two main features of Newtown are the large and not especially attractive headquarters of the Scottish Borders Council and the auction mart where sheep and cattle are regularly sold. The council offices, by Peter Womersley, won an architectural competition in the 1960s, but the complex is described in a modern architectural guide as "dominating the village by virtue of its squat cathedral-like scale and utter disregard for its neighbours".

Other buildings of note include the 1888 Baillie Hall, constructed in memory of Major the Honourable Robert Baillie, described on the plaque as being "a man full of faith and of the Holy Ghost". Clearly a Christian soldier. The Railway Hotel is a pleasant Victorian sandstone construction. The railway, as indicated above, has long gone. Despite its name, Newtown is old enough, and is named as such on maps of the 17th century.

On reaching the main road, cross straight over and climb slightly to another road. Cross this also (follow the sign

'Footpath to the River'). Go through an area of garages and sheds and then right, down a path and under the huge modern road viaduct carrying the A68. Continue down the attractive small glen, keeping on its right-hand side, to join the Tweed footpath. It may be surprising to learn that there is a thriving population of otters on the Tweed and its tributaries, but you will still be very lucky to spot one of these beautiful creatures.

Go right along the footpath and follow it above the river. You pass behind Tweed Horizons, a large white-towered building that was previously a religious seminary called St Columba's. It is now a centre for innovative and sustainable industries and experimentation, run by Scottish Enterprise Borders (SEB). Soon afterwards you reach a lovely viewpoint with a seat looking back up the Tweed, and then drop down steps to the lane end at the Dryburgh footbridge.

A short diversion from here across the river would enable you to visit **Dryburgh Abbey**. This is another superb ruin, of a foundation of Premonstratensians which dates back to 1150. The monks, also known as White Canons, are believed to have come here from Alnwick in Northumberland. They could hardly have chosen a more perfect and peaceful site, in a secluded bend of the Tweed.

The Abbey's chapter-house contains traces of the earliest painted ceiling in Scotland. It is common to assume that, when first built, these religious houses were sombre if majestic places, but in fact many of them contained riotously colourful decoration on the walls, pillars and ceilings. The Abbey holds the grave of Sir Walter Scott and other members of his family, and also of Field Marshal Earl Haig, the Army commander from World War One, whose family home is at nearby Bemersyde.

Another interesting diversion is to walk up the hill through the village from the Abbey and turn left as signed along the path to the large sandstone statue of William Wallace. This extraordinary, massive figure, 8m high with shield and huge sword, was carved in 1814 by John Smith, commissioned by the Earl of Buchan. In more recent times, woodland growth meant that the statue was half-hidden, but following an appeal involving among others

Dryburgh Abbey.

the Saltire Society, it has been brought back to full view, repaired and cleaned. Apparently the statue was originally painted white, which must have looked very peculiar. Since the release of the film *Braveheart* about Wallace's life, the statue has become much better known and more popular with visitors.

Return over the footbridge, noting the charming Temple of the Muses, a gazebo topped by a bust of James Thomson, the Border poet, and containing bronze sculptures celebrating his work, *The Seasons*.

Continue with the path beside the Tweed. There is usually a good variety of birdlife on this section of the river, including dipper, mute swan, moorhen, mallard and heron. All sections of the river are named as fishing beats: the first sections passed after the Dryburgh footbridge were simply Cauld Pool and Cauld Stream, and you now walk beside Harecraig Stream to Burnfoot Pool.

The Tweed at Dryburgh.

The river swings round a long and fairly tight bend, one of a number it takes in this area, and its flow has meant that bank stabilisation has been necessary in recent years. Despite this, there is one section where the path is forced through a narrow rocky gap. In winter or spring, when the river is especially full, this section can flood. If this is the case, the only alternative is to walk the road between Newtown and St Boswells. Although it is the main A68, there is a pavement all the way.

Between the rocky gap and St Boswells, the path climbs and dips with several flights of steps and footbridges over small burns, before dropping to the river bank, crossing another footbridge and then climbing quite steeply to enter St Boswells village.

St Boswells has facilities that include public toilets and shops selling food and drink. Across the A68, to your right, is the Buccleuch Arms Hotel where more substantial refreshments can be found if needed, and beside the hotel is the 16-hectare village green, a rather English-looking feature for a Scottish village; it even has a cricket pitch.

The green was at one time the site of a yearly horse fair, and the tradition lingers with an annual gathering of travelling folk each July; motor caravans are more common than horses nowadays, not unnaturally. It was from such horse fairs that the term 'horse trading' came. Originally it simply meant 'hard bargaining', but it has now come to mean something rather more dubious.

St Boswells takes its name from St Boisil, who was Cuthbert's early mentor at Melrose. Notable buildings in the village include the parish church of 1836 by John and Thomas Smith. It has good modern stained glass by Liz Rowley. It became the village's church as recently as 1952, when the former church at Benrig ceased to be used. There is still a large cemetery at Benrig. The village hall, dated on its weathervane to 1892, is typical of its period.

2
ST BOSWELLS TO HARESTANES

SUMMARY

Distance: 12km (7.5 miles).

Height Range: 70-170m.

Accommodation: Hotel and B&Bs in St Boswells, B&Bs in Ancrum (1 km west of Harestanes). Campsite at Lilliardsedge (1 km off route).

Food and Drink: Available in St Boswells, Woodside Garden Centre (100m off route), Harestanes Visitor Centre (closed in winter) and in Ancrum.

Public Transport: Regular bus services to St Boswells from Edinburgh and Jedburgh passing near Harestanes Visitor Centre (800m west).

Terrain Summary: A walk alongside the Tweed to Maxton before joining the course of the Roman Dere Street which crosses an undulating landscape. The day ends with an attractive woodland walk.

Before leaving St Boswells, you might like to reflect on the fact that the annual horse fair (where much else was traded besides horses) was sufficiently important for the poet James Hogg, known as the Ettrick Shepherd, to decline an invitation from his monarch, King George III, to visit him in London. Hogg's reason was that, as a tenant farmer, it would not do for him to miss the St Boswells Fair – the king put firmly in his place!

To continue the walk from St Boswells, walk east along the main street of the village and turn left at Braeheads Road. On the far corner across the road as you turn left there is a small drinking fountain which bears the rather off-putting inscription: "Jesus said whosoever drinketh of this water shall thirst again, but whosoever drinketh of the water that I give him shall never thirst". The fountain is on the corner of Jean Lawrie Court, named after a much-loved local historian and schoolteacher who died not so many years ago.

St Boswells Golf Course.

Climb the hill and at the top go right with the road above the golf course, then left, down to and past the golf clubhouse. From the upper road there is a lovely view looking across the river to the Eildon Hills. St Boswells Golf Club was founded here in 1899. The attractive 9-hole course runs along by the river on an area of ground known as Great Stenhouse, and is always very well kept. When using the path here, please take care, although for most of the time you are on a bank and out of the way of stray shots. The club has kindly said that walkers can use the clubhouse facilities, which include not only toilets, but also (when open) a bar.

At the fence corner below the clubhouse, turn right as waymarked and follow the fence closely right along the edge of the golf course – on a bank for most of the way on a good walking surface. At the far end of the course there are two pieces of ground known as The Anna and The Indies. Continue on the path (Birkiehaugh Stream here) as it follows the river bank round a sweeping bend with notable eroded sandstone pillars on the opposite bank. You soon pass a weir, with Caul Pool above it, to reach Mertoun Bridge, a fine red sandstone construction. It dates to 1841 and was designed by James Sleight.

Across the river is the former Mertoun Mill by the weir with its central gap to encourage water flow, which helps the fishing. Salmon making their way upriver to spawn leap this gap each autumn. You will often see fishermen here during the season – the attractive cottage near the former mill is let out by Mertoun Estate to anglers. Salmon fishing has long been important to the Borders economy, and the Tweed is one of the finest of all Scotland's salmon rivers.

Go up steps, cross the road with care and go down steps again to regain the path. Continue along the riverside, a lovely stretch called Fens Haugh with good birdlife, which may include goosanders as well as the commoner birds. Herons are frequently seen on this section. Note the splendid rows of tall poplars across the river on the Mertoun Estate, which is owned by the Duke of Sutherland. The path enters woodland at The Pot and continues below Benrig House, passing the Crystal Well which has been renovated. There is a surprising amount of up and down on this section, but all on well-constructed steps.

Mertoun Bridge.

This is another section with a good range of mature trees, including beech, oak, elm and lime as well as some conifers. The path meanders through the wood, down to the river bank and up again, and all told this is a truly delightful stretch of the walk and not to be hurried over. You pass just behind the old Benrig Cemetery, drop down to cross a track used by fishermen to gain riverside access and eventually go up a long flight of steps to emerge by Maxton Church, another fine old building of simple design. It has some 17th century work, but is mainly from the mid-18th century. Its bell is Dutch and dates from 1609. The church is still regularly used for worship and is the only church dedicated to St Cuthbert passed on St Cuthbert's Way.

Turn right up the lane into Maxton village. At the time of writing it lacked both shop and pub. Maxton claims to have been the birthplace of the medieval scholar John Duns Scotus, more often associated with the Berwickshire town of Duns which became part of his name.

The Maxton version of the story is that Scotus was born at Littledean Tower, which overlooks the Tweed a little east of the village, in about 1265. After entering the priesthood as a Franciscan in Northampton, Scotus taught religion at the universities of Oxford and Paris, and later in Cologne, where he died in 1308. During the Renaissance, those who followed his teaching were called 'Dunses', a mocking term meaning obstinate, and by association stupid, and it is from this that our word 'dunce' is said to come – an odd linguistic association for a small Borders village.

Go right at the main road and then first left. Follow this road across the old railway and round several bends for 1km, and immediately before the A68 road is reached, turn left onto Dere Street. This Roman road continues straight ahead for 5km, with minor diversions around a plantation, some houses and a sawmill. The path is waymarked along Dere Street with a Roman helmet throughout, as well as SCW signs at significant points. It is not really possible to lose the way, but if in doubt, follow the Roman helmets.

It is at first a clear path between fences, but later becomes open pasture. Please keep to the edge of the fields to avoid damage to any grass (silage) crop. Silage or hay

Lady Lilliard's Stone.

may be cut to provide food for livestock. Later the route is fenced in again as it runs through woodland and scrub, which can become rather overgrown in summer.

Just past the top of a rise, a short diversion to the right through a gate will enable you to see Lady Lilliard's Stone, a small coffin-shaped monument to the legendary bravery of a local woman during the Battle of Ancrum Moor, fought in this area in 1545. The inscription records that:

> *Fair Maiden Lilliard lies under this stane*
> *Little was her stature, but muckle was her fame*
> *Upon the English loons she laid many thumps,*
> *And when her legs were cuttit off, she fought upon her*
> *   stumps.*

A doughty lady indeed. Ancrum Moor was fought between the English army commanded by Sir Ralph Evers and Sir Brian Laiton, who had pillaged much of the surrounding area, and the Scots force of the Earl of Angus and Scott of Buccleuch. It was a resounding victory for the 'home side', the Scots slaughtering 800 of the English and taking a further 1,000 as prisoners. It is recorded that Ker and Turnbull 'mercenaries' who had joined up with the English changed sides when they saw how the battle was going. The term 'freelance', used today to indicate someone working for themselves, comes from those times. It was used for groups of fighting men, or mercenaries, who could be hired. They were not attached to any particular clan or family and as part of their standard armoury was a lance, they were called the 'free lances'.

There was also apparently a 'magna petra' or 'great stone' called Lilyot's Cross here in early medieval times, erected by the monks of Melrose to mark a boundary. The cross was later used as a place for meetings between the Wardens of the Scottish and English Marches on 'truce days' to resolve disputes and dispense Border justice regarding such matters as stolen goods or livestock, compensation for killings, or family feuds – not easy matters

Dere Street from Lilliardsedge.

Down Law and Baron's Folly.

to arbitrate on. If no peaceful settlement was possible, then trial by combat was not infrequently ordered.

If you are intending to stop overnight at the Lilliardsedge Campsite, you will need to leave the path here and cross to the A68. Cross this busy road with care to reach the campsite. On a small hill above the campsite, and clearly visible from Dere Street, is the Monteath Mausoleum, erected in memory of Sir Thomas Monteath Douglas of Stonebyres in Lanarkshire after his death in 1868.

Dere Street originally ran from York all the way to the Forth near Edinburgh. This is one of the best-preserved stretches and can in fact be walked all the way to the English border. The route was for long known as Agricola's Road, after the Roman governor during whose period in Britain (AD 79-83) it was made. The armies constructing the road set up a number of camps which can still be traced on the ground. The route followed today is not always exactly on the original line of Dere Street, but it is never far off it, and it is remarkable how well the line of the route has survived over nearly 2000 years. St Cuthbert would certainly have known this route as it would have been one of the few well-made roads anywhere in the area.

After Lilliard's Stone, the route continues across fairly open ground between fences. To the left is Down Law, crowned by a small building known as the Baron's Folly.

It is said that it was used by the baron in question for a spot of amorous dalliance while a servant kept watch in case the Baroness decided to come this way! Below the hill on its south side is Baron's Folly Moss, a large wetland area with a variable amount of standing water. It is home to a considerable variety of waders in spring and autumn, including redshank, ruff and curlew, and to duck and geese in winter.

You eventually cross a minor road and enter the Monteviot estate woodland through a small gate. Follow the path down through Divet Ha' Wood. The tall tower seen on the left at one point is used for shooting roe deer, which you might see here. The woods are also used for pheasant-rearing, and shoots take place in the late autumn and early winter after the visitor centre has closed for the season. Straw is often spread on the woodland rides as the pheasants like to scratch in it, and they congregate in large numbers to do so.

Follow the signs across the Marble Burn and then turn right to walk down beside the burn (a signposted path on the right leads to the Woodside Garden Centre with its café – 100m off route) and then cross a minor road. You are now joining the Harestanes waymarked walks system, which uses coloured arrows. Dere Street is clearly signposted: the route here is not actually that of the Roman Road but is a negotiated route for walkers through Monteviot Estate. A short diversion leads to the Harestanes Countryside Visitor Centre, which has exhibitions, shop, toilets and a tearoom. The Centre is run by Scottish Borders Council and is open from 1 April to 31 October. Housed in a former farm steading, it started its new life in the 1970s as a Woodland Centre run by Lothian Estates. It also houses the Council's Countryside Ranger Service, who provide an extensive programme of guided walks throughout the Borders all year round. Information and refreshments are available at the Centre.

A popular walk from the Centre leads up to the Waterloo Monument on Peniel Heugh, a notable Borders viewpoint seen from a wide area. The monument, by Archibald Elliot, was begun in 1815, collapsed during construction the following year, but was rebuilt and finally completed in 1824. It is typical of many of its period to be found all over Britain. The timber viewing

Harestanes Countryside Visitor Centre.

platform was added in 1867. A plaque records that 'To the Duke of Wellington and the British Army, William Kerr, VI Marquis of Lothian and his Tenantry dedicated this monument'.

The monument was extensively restored in 1994-95 with the assistance of a grant from Historic Scotland. Entry is restricted at the time of writing, but there is still a fine view extending almost around 360 degrees from the foot of the monument. The eye is drawn back to the Eildons, near the start of St Cuthbert's Way, and onward to the Cheviots, which have still to be crossed as the route makes progress towards England.

If you are ending your stage at Harestanes, the nearest accommodation is in Ancrum, 1km to the west, or in Jedburgh, further away but with more choice. The next section of the route in fact comes within 3km of Jedburgh which can then be reached by following the Borders Abbeys Way.

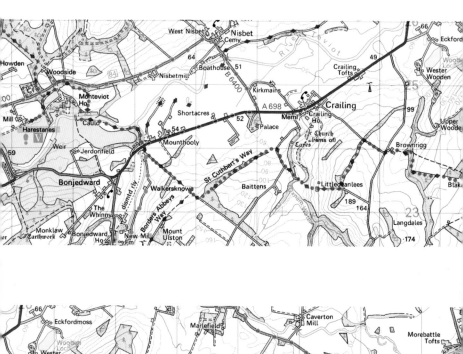

3
HARESTANES TO MOREBATTLE

SUMMARY

Distance: 16km (10 miles).

Height Range: 50-190m.

Accommodation: B&Bs in Ancrum, hotels and B&Bs in Jedburgh (2.5km off route) and Morebattle.

Food and Drink: Available at Harestanes Visitor Centre (not in winter), Mounthooly (300m east of the route at Jedfoot Bridge) and Morebattle.

Public Transport: Regular buses from Edinburgh and Jedburgh pass near Harestanes. From Morebattle to Kelso, buses daily except Sundays.

Terrain Summary: After crossing the River Teviot this section goes through a typical Borders landscape with attractive stretches of woodland, the deep valley of the Oxnam Water and a crossing of Cessford Moor. A walk along a quiet country road brings you into Morebattle.

If not visiting Harestanes, or to return to the route from the Centre, follow Dere Street signs until you pick up the SCW waymarking again. On the way you cross the main drive to Monteviot House. Seat of the Earls of Ancrum and earlier Earls of Lothian, it dates back to 1740, but was substantially rebuilt and enlarged in 1840 to a design by Edward Blore, whose other work included Sir Walter Scott's house at Abbotsford, near Melrose. He was also one of the architects for Buckingham Palace in London. The gardens of Monteviot House, which were redesigned in the 1960s by Percy Cane, are open to the public in summer.

A 17th century Earl of Lothian, while away fighting with a Covenanting army, sent a message home to his father, the Marquess: "I must trouble your Lordship to desire that I might have two nightcaps and two pair of slippers, one grass green, the other sky colour, with gold or silver lace upon them". Warfare must have been a more civilised process in those times.

Continue through the Monteviot Estate to cross the
River Teviot by a long suspension bridge. The previous
bridge was badly damaged in the severe floods of Feb-
ruary 1997 and its replacement was opened in 1999. Just
before the bridge a large but ruinous dovecot can be seen
among the trees. Many estates had these dovecots in past
times, the birds (several hundred in the larger buildings)
providing meat at times when other sources were scarce.
This one shows evidence of 17th century origins, but was
enlarged 200 years later. It is worth noting that this area
of woodland contains a number of hornbeam, a fairly
uncommon tree.

At the far side of the Teviot, turn left and walk along
the river bank to the confluence with the Jed Water. Turn
right and follow the path to the main road. Cross with care
and go left over the Jed Water, turn right and then half-left
to pick up Dere Street again (very clear, arrowing away
uphill dead straight). Please note that from here to Tow-
ford, Dere Street is still legally a vehicular right of way,
although for most of the distance it is unsurfaced. You
may therefore encounter motorcycles and also horses; the
track is used quite often by farm vehicles too.

It appears that the Romans may have deviated from
their normal practice in that Dere Street probably crossed
both the Jed Water and the Teviot. Normally, when faced
with two rivers so close together, the practice would be to
move the crossing to the major river after it had received
the tributary. The reason for the double crossing is not
known.

The exact line of Dere Street through the Monteviot
Estate is in fact unclear. The land here has been cultivated
or planted with trees for centuries and the line of the Roman road is lost. It has been suggested that the drive of
Monteviot House is on the line of the road, and also that
there might have been a small guardpost at the crossing
of the Teviot, which would be understandable.

On Dere Street, St Cuthbert's Way is joined by the
Borders Abbeys Way for a short distance. At the top of
the first rise, the Borders Abbeys Way goes to the right
towards Jedburgh, some 3km distant. St Cuthbert's Way
continues on Dere Street for a further 200m. As mentioned
earlier, historians assure us that St Cuthbert himself
would certainly have known of Dere Street, and probably

The Bridge over Oxnam Water.

used it, as it was one of the very few made roads at that time. It is amazing that it has survived to the present day so remarkably well.

At the waymark, turn left into a belt of woodland along a clear path. This attractive path meanders through broadleaf woods with excellent views over Teviotdale and to the Waterloo Monument on Peniel Heugh. After about 1.5km the path leaves the wood and turns right along the road. When the road bends right, bear left along a grassy track. After a bend in the track the path descends steeply to cross the Oxnam Water by a foot-bridge. Looking back to your left you will see the red sandstone cliffs above the bend in the river. Walk up across the field to a gate in the fence. Continue climbing to reach a waymark by a grassy track, where you turn left and ascend towards a wood. Before the wood, the track bends right to follow the fence uphill to reach the cottage of Littledeanlees.

The path keeps well to the right of the cottage and passes through a wicket gate out onto a private road. Follow this

View from Cessford.

road uphill towards the belt of trees on the skyline. At the top of the hill, a wicket gate on the left leads into another delightful woodland path with even more extensive views than on the earlier path. When the path reaches a road, turn right to a T-junction. Turn left towards the buildings of Brownrigg. Before reaching the first cottage, go through a wicket gate on the right onto a field edge path leading downhill past a derelict stone barn. At the foot of the hill, cross a footbridge and keep to the left-hand edge of the next field, heading towards a wooded valley.

Turn right above the valley towards mature woodland ahead. Enter the woods and descend to cross the burn below and climb up towards the edge of the woods. Veer right and keep inside the wood which now levels out. At the end of the wood, go through the gate in the wall to your left and then turn right towards another wood. Cross a footbridge and enter this wood, keeping to its right-hand edge. On leaving this wood, go straight ahead following the wall and bear left with it. To your right is an isolated rock outcrop known as Blakeman's Crag.

At the top of a slight rise, a step-stile on the right takes you towards a further wood along a field edge path. On reaching the wood, turn sharp left, then sharp right along the left-hand edge of the wood. As you approach a main track, a superb panorama of the Cheviots opens up. Turn left onto the track and follow it along and then round to the right to descend to Cessford, with more beautiful views of the Cheviot Hills with Cessford Castle in the foreground.

Cessford is now just a large farm and a group of cottages, but there was formerly a more considerable settlement here, and it is worth pausing for a moment to consider the recent history of the place. The story of the community here is very typical of many rural areas of Scotland. In the 1841 Census, the 'Barony of Cessford', which still took in only the immediate area, listed no fewer than 258 people, including a blacksmith, joiner, builder, mason and teacher. Up to the end of the 18th century there would have been many scattered smallholdings here. Then, when the Enclosure Acts were passed, the larger farmers who held title to the land did not renew the smallholders' leases. This led to a situation almost like the Highland Clearances. The ministers who wrote descriptions of the Borders parishes for the *First Statistical Account*, published in 1793, are consistent in their view that at this time there were many more paupers than previously, and that many small houses were demolished.

Before this time, the main group of cottages at Cessford had been in the lee of the castle walls, extending north to the point where the road bends sharply. The land came into the ownership of the MacDougall family, and the *New Statistical Account* of 1834 records that "Mr MacDougall has cleared away all the scattered cottages at Cessford and replaced them with one neat row".

These houses, built in 1821, were alongside the stone wall that now marks the eastern end of the cottage gardens. The smithy, joiner's workshop and school were in the large hollow, or dene. The present row of cottages was built in the 1870s.

The track that you have just walked over is shown on Stobbie's map of 1760 as the main road from Wooler to Jedburgh. It continued down into the dene, forded the burn, and climbed the far side to run past the castle. The MacDougalls seem to have changed the road pattern, probably to give an easier crossing of the dene and its burn.

Old maps record a number of farm names that have now disappeared. Essex Mains was a separate holding above Cessford, at the point where the track bends sharply west. Bowhouses was approximately where Cessford Farmhouse is now, and eighteen people are recorded as living there. 'Bow', quite a common place-name element in the Borders, seems to be associated with cattle. Shankfoot was down in the dene and is shown as 'previously known as Priestcroft', perhaps indicating that a minister either lived or held services there. There is no record of a church at Cessford.

Well into this century, the community here was much more self-sufficient than it is today. The joiner, clearly a fine craftsman, made carts for customers as far away as Berwick. The blacksmith repaired the carts and shod both their horses and the many horses used on the farms, which included Burn Farm, Tan Law and Marchcleuch. The village name, according to some records, was originally Cesseworthe, meaning 'the settlement by the peat bog'.

At a triangle of grass at the entrance to Cessford Farm, turn left to walk up past the castle. This imposing structure, an L-plan fortified tower, was a stronghold of the Kers and was built in the mid-15th century. The Kers (another branch, spelling their name Kerr, was based at Ferniehirst, near Jedburgh) were major players in the reiving times, when there was an almost constant battle back and forth across the Border.

Cessford saw its share of conflict. It was attacked by English forces four times between 1519 and 1544. The Earl of Surrey described it as "the third strongest castle in Scotland". The castle, very typical of its period, was designed to withstand regular assault while giving the maximum protection, but not necessarily particular comfort, to those inside.

Many of the Kers were left-handed, and a dialect word 'kerry-pawed' survived until recent times. In the early

Cessford Castle.

17th century, Sir Robert Ker was made Warden of the Middle Marches, giving him responsibility for keeping the peace over the whole area. He acquired the title of Lord Roxburghe. In time the heads of the family became Dukes, and the castle is today still in the hands of Roxburghe Estates, whose head, the present Duke, lives at the magnificent Floors Castle near Kelso, the largest inhabited house in Scotland. His ancestor Robert Ker was known as Habbie or Hobbie, and you can still find Hobbie Ker's Cave, no doubt a handy hiding place, marked on OS maps near Cessford today. The Ferniehirst Kerrs eventually became Marquesses of Lothian, so between them these two branches of one family still hold much of the land in this area.

As well as major incursions by English and Scottish forces there were innumerable more local feuds involving cattle-rustling, theft and occupation of property, taking of prisoners and other manly pursuits. Today we frequently use the term 'caught red-handed', which comes from reiving times. Anyone coming home and finding that a raid had taken place and that, say, his cattle had been taken, would commonly round up as many men as he could find quickly and set off in pursuit of the raiding party. This was called a 'hot trod'. If the raiders were caught before reaching safety, those who had been wronged were allowed to take immediate, and often bloody, revenge. Hence the raiding party were literally 'caught red-handed'.

In recent years stabilising work has been done on the castle and, although it is still dangerous to enter the building, the outside can be closely inspected from the surrounding field, and an interpretive panel has been erected nearby.

You can perhaps muse on the rich history of this small place as you tackle the road section which follows: it is hard on the feet but there is compensation in the fine views ahead to the Cheviot Hills. Keep with the road round several bends for 2.5km, passing the lodge for Otterburn House, to meet the B6401. Turn right and walk along the road for 1km into Morebattle, another neat Borders village with inn, shops and public toilets. Just before reaching the village you may notice a series of small fields on the right of the road. These are called The Polmers, and are leased by villagers from the Church

Morebattle village.

of Scotland's Glasgow Diocese. Behind them is the large farm of Morebattle Mains.

On the way into Morebattle you pass the thriving village school on the left and then the charmingly-named Teapot Street. The parish church dates from 1757. There were at one time three churches in Morebattle. One of them is now converted to serve as the village hall (on the right just before the crossroads, with public toilets next to it). This church was previously sited at Hownam, 6km south of Morebattle, and was moved here stone by stone.

The shop, which sells a good range of refreshments, is on the left just before the crossroads. Once over the crossroads the road dips and you pass Morebattle's pub, the Templehall Inn, which welcomes walkers and also provides overnight accommodation and meals if needed.

4
MOREBATTLE TO KIRK YETHOLM

SUMMARY

Distance: 11 km (6.5 miles).

Height Range: 90-368 m.

Accommodation: Hotels and B&Bs in Morebattle, Town Yetholm and Kirk Yetholm, Youth Hostel in Kirk Yetholm.

Food and Drink: Available in Morebattle, Town Yetholm and Kirk Yetholm.

Public Transport: Morebattle and Kirk Yetholm are served by bus to and from Kelso (not Sundays).

Terrain Summary: This section is the most strenuous of the whole route. It includes a sustained climb to nearly 400m (1300 feet) on Wideopen Hill, with a number of steep sections, before descending into the Bowmont Valley. The compensation is the fabulous views obtained in clear conditions.

The alternative is to walk the road between Morebattle and Yetholm. This alternative is recommended during very severe weather conditions such as heavy snow, or in mist if you are unsure of your navigational skills.

Leave Morebattle by the Yetholm road but take the first turning right, signed to Hownam (pronounced Hoonam). The road climbs over a low ridge and then drops into the Kale Water valley; the road here is called Sibbald's Path. The name Morebattle does not have warlike origins: it is in fact from 'mere botle', meaning 'the settlement by the lake'. What lake, you may wonder? Well, at the top of the ridge on the minor road, looking left, you can see Linton Church on its mound. The ground in front of it was drained only relatively recently, and was for long marked as Linton Loch, though it was more of a marsh. The original wetland area extended north-west as far as Caverton Mill. Linton itself means 'the farm by the lake'.

This was the home of the fabled Linton worm, a dragon which caused great havoc and distress in the

Kale Footbridge.

area in medieval times. It was finally defeated by Sir John Somerville, who would, it seems, have put 'dragon slaying' as his profession if asked, for he seemed to make something of a speciality of this art. Linton Church dates back to the 12th century, and has lovely modern stained glass.

Before the last Ice Age, about 12,000 years ago, the Kale flowed north-east towards Yetholm. As the glaciers in this area melted, the Kale ate its way through the soft sandstone – a good example of 'river capture'.

At a road junction, turn right and walk alongside the Kale Water. After 400m pass a ford on the left and after a further 100m cross a footbridge over the river, leaving the road behind – no doubt with some relief.

Cross the field to a clear track, turn right along it and follow it as it bears left above a small quarry to a crossing track. Keep straight ahead, uphill, bearing left and climbing steadily with a burn and fence on your right. Continue uphill to the end of the field. Turn right over a stile and walk up the field edge, using the boardwalk to cross two ditches. At the top of the field go through the gate and continue straight ahead, uphill. The path continues to climb with ever widening views to left and right.

Looking back, you can see Morebattle spread below you and all the Border country extending to the Eildons and round to the right towards the distant Lammermuir Hills on the boundary between Berwickshire and East Lothian. To the west, the prominent hill of Rubers Law stands out – it has an Iron Age fort on its summit. Southwards, Hownam Law stands out above the valley of the Kale Water, and you can often see the ramparts of its summit fort.

When a crossing path is reached, turn left and continue climbing around the summit of Grubbit Law. Its name comes from an old personal name, Grub or Grubb. (A short detour to its summit is recommended.) Go straight ahead towards a wall and keep alongside it to a ladder stile on the skyline. Cross this stile which is at a junction of two walls. Since crossing the Kale Water you have been on the ground of Playfair Farms, but here you cross back into Roxburghe Estates. Keep ahead following the wall to the summit of Wideopen Hill, at 368m the highest point on the Way and also approximately the halfway point.

Its name is appropriate: there are more great views here – ahead to the Cheviots this time and down half-left to the twin Yetholm villages, with Yetholm Loch prominent over to their left. Directly below is the Bowmont Valley, which you will now drop down into. The wall bends sharp right and then left and descends quite steeply. Cross another wall by a stile and keep ahead, going left, right, left with the main wall along the ridge over Crookedshaws Hill, descending steadily. Keep following the wall to a small gate. Go through the gate, continue downhill, turn right over a stile and then cross the field and go over another stile on the left.

Walk down the field, with its odd small clump of trees, and cross the stile onto Old Crookedshaws Lane. 'Shaw' in any placename indicates a wood. Turn right and walk down the disused lane to the road. Turn left and follow the road and the Bowmont Water to Primsidemill. This attractive name means 'the mill house by the white wood'. Continue straight ahead at the crossroads and at the B6401

Back Dykes, Yetholm.

turn right towards Yetholm. This road has a good grass verge to walk on.

After 600m pass a small cemetery and turn right into a lane. After 50m go left along an old track between trees. This is called the Back Dykes and can be followed right into Yetholm, passing Romany House on the left. Between the track and the house is a wetland area with a large sheet of water, home to a variety of birds including ducks, swans, waders and grebes.

The track goes through two gates enclosing an area sometimes used for gathering livestock. This area, and the section beyond it, can become very muddy, especially in winter when cattle are grazed on the haugh. Cross the haugh, aiming just left of the square electricity pylon, and, with the Bowmont Water on your right, reach the road at a gate. Turn right to cross the fine old Yetholm Bridge.

After crossing the bridge go left down steps at its far side. Follow the clear path going ahead across the haugh, then turn right through a gate and into the lane leading

Opposite: Bowmont Valley.

to the youth hostel. If you look left from the gate you will see the now disused Blunty's Mill, once renowned for the production of blankets. Just before the youth hostel there is a charming little stone bridge on the left that appears to be completely redundant!

Continue past the youth hostel and up to the large village green with the Border Hotel and its sign proclaiming 'End of the Pennine Way' on the left.

If you wish to go into Town Yetholm, for accommodation or supplies, there is a path from the haugh running up left into the village centre, which consists of a fine broad street with lovely mature trees. Yetholm takes its name from its position, only a short distance from the border with England. The name means 'the gate town', yett being an old Scots word for a gate or doorway.

This is a peaceful and attractive place today, but as with all the Border villages, it saw conflict in the troubled times. In 1545, when the Earl of Hertford led the series of raids called the 'Rough Wooing', Yetholm was on his list of places to be burned and pillaged.

The Border Hotel at the end of the Pennine Way.

Yetholm was a 'farm township', with a large number of thatched houses, of which one or two are still maintained. Even the parish church was thatched until replaced by the present rather sombre building, designed by Robert Brown, in 1836. Many of the older buildings still have their barn as an outbuilding and until recent times many families kept a 'house cow' on the haugh to provide milk. The monument on the green is to the memory of Major-General Andrew Wauchope, who died in the Boer War in South Africa in 1899. The Wauchopes remain prominent landowners in the area today.

Perhaps the most famous association for Yetholm, however, is with the gypsy folk, going back at least as far as 1695. Tradition states that during a battle in France a soldier with gypsy origins saved the life of a British officer, Captain Bennet. The Captain had land in the Yetholm area and as a mark of gratitude made this and some cottages in the village available to his saviour and descendants. The youth hostel was originally built as a school for gypsy children.

For many years, gypsies gathered in Yetholm to elect a King and Queen and to hold a coronation. The Faa family supplied many of these gypsy 'monarchs', and Esther Faa Blythe, who died in 1883, is said to have been the last Queen of the Gypsies. Another famous gypsy was Jean Gordon. Born in Yetholm, she inspired the character of Meg Merrilees in Walter Scott's novel *Guy Mannering*.

By the beginning of the 20th century the gypsy way of life was dying out. Many settled and integrated into the community, and if you go into Yetholm Church you will see stained glass windows donated by Andrew Blythe, a former church elder who was of gypsy descent.

The gypsy tradition is kept alive each summer with the election of a young man and woman as the Bari Gadgi and Bari Manushi. They preside over the celebrations during Yetholm's Civic Week, and provide us with a link to the long history of the gypsies, the Romany folk, in the Yetholm area.

5
KIRK YETHOLM TO HETHPOOL

SUMMARY
Distance: 8km (5 miles).
Height Range: 110-340m.
Accommodation: Hotels and B&Bs in Town and Kirk Yetholm, B&B in Hethpool.
Food and Drink: Available in Town and Kirk Yetholm only.
Public Transport: Bus service Kelso–Kirk Yetholm only (not on Sundays).
Terrain Summary: A 1.5 km long road walk to the Halterburn Valley, then a steady climb onto the Border Ridge followed by a gradual descent to Elsdonburn. A 2km walk along a farm road ends this section.

From the green at Kirk Yetholm, follow the signs up the road towards Halterburn. This part of the route is also the final section of the Pennine Way, which ends its long journey from Edale in Derbyshire at Kirk Yetholm. The road climbs to give good views down the Bowmont Valley. After 1.5km, at a large grassy area, leave the road to go left across a small burn and climb on a clear path and then track (still the Pennine Way). Leave the track as waymarked about 400m before the Pennine Way meets the Border fence and wall, to go half left across a dip then over a rise and up to a gate in the Border fence and wall with its twin signs saying 'Welcome to England' and 'Welcome to Scotland'.

Go through the gate to join a clear path heading over the col directly ahead. A short diversion on the left to the summit of Eccles Cairn will be rewarded with a splendid view across the Border hills – and a last look back at the Eildons, which have been in view for most of the way up to now. The prominent hills seen close by are Coldsmouth Hill to the north, crowned with Bronze Age burial cairns and, on the Scottish side of the Border,

Signpost at the border between Scotland and England.

Burnt Humbleton and Green Humbleton, each with an iron age hillfort, the ramparts of which can clearly be seen when the light is right.

The path descends towards Tuppies Sike Burn. At the foot of the slope, boggy ground has to be negotiated before crossing the burn and climbing slightly to enter the wood ahead over a stile. The path emerges into daylight and follows a fence before re-entering the wood.

On leaving the wood over a stile, walk straight ahead across the field to a gate. Cross a burn onto a farm track which keeps above the burn round a bend to drop down to Elsdonburn Farm. Turn left after the bungalow, cross a bridge and go right along the metalled road.

After 900m this road is joined by another descending from Trowupburn Farm, which lies 2km to the south. In medieval times Trowupburn was a grange of Melrose Abbey. The abbey's considerable wealth came from its vast flocks of sheep kept on the Cheviot Hills and elsewhere in the Borders. Many of the fleeces were exported to the wool merchants of Flanders. The hills seen to the right are Little and Great Hetha, each crowned with an Iron Age hillfort.

A kilometre along the road you reach a gate. Look up to the hill on your left here to see the cultivation terraces on the flank of White Hill. These could well be of prehistoric origin and they continued in use well into post-medieval times. The wooded hill facing you is Hethpool Bell, and the trees on its flank are known as the Collingwood Oaks. They were planted by Admiral Lord Collingwood, Nelson's second-in-command, who owned the estate at the time, to provide timber for the great warships known as 'the wooden walls of England'. Unfortunately he had not taken into account the Cheviot winds and the poor soil. The trees grew very slowly and became stunted, but fortunately the Navy had invested in iron-clad ships before they reached maturity.

Lord Collingwood was born in Newcastle in 1750. He entered the Navy as a boy of 11 and first served with Nelson in 1778. From then on, their careers followed parallel paths. He was involved in the battles off Brest in 1794 and at Cape St Vincent in 1797 before acting as Nelson's second-in-command at Trafalgar in 1805. He died at sea in 1819 and is buried beside Nelson in St Paul's Cathedral in London. Appropriately for this walk, Collingwood's Christian name was Cuthbert.

Turn right after closing the gate, passing the entrance to Hethpool House on the left, and continue to the bend

Elsdonburn Farm.

Hethpool Cottages.

in the road. The delightful cottages here were designed by Robert Mauchlin in the Arts & Crafts style and date from 1926. Mauchlin also worked on additions to the big house.

THE COLLEGE VALLEY

This beautiful, unspoilt valley is owned by the Sir James Knott Trust, a philanthropic body set up by the Tyneside shipping magnate who died in 1934. The trust maintains a policy of welcoming walkers and others seeking quiet recreation. Motor traffic is restricted by only allowing twelve cars per day to proceed beyond Hethpool by permit, with a complete ban on cars during the lambing season in April and May.

The College Burn follows the course of a geological fault line, which during the Ice Age was scoured out by the ice flowing from Cheviot's summit. Originating on the western side of the Cheviot, the burn descends through the gorge known as the Hen Hole into the valley bottom to flow eventually into the Bowmont Water at Westnewton, to form the River Glen.

The valley contains a number of working sheep farms and areas of commercial forestry, within which three large coniferous plantations have been felled and replanted with deciduous trees. On the lower slopes of Harelaw, just south of Hethpool, a large area of ancient birch and hazel woodland has survived and is now designated as a Site of Special Scientific Interest by Natural England.

At the head of the valley, at Mounthooly, the trust has installed a bunkhouse in a redundant farm building, and this is available to both groups and individuals at a small overnight charge; it is now affiliated to the YHA. The name College does not refer to an educational establishment, or even the more fanciful interpretation of the name as a haunt of a college or coven of witches. It most probably derives from the Anglo-Saxon 'col' and 'leche', meaning a stream flowing through marshy ground.

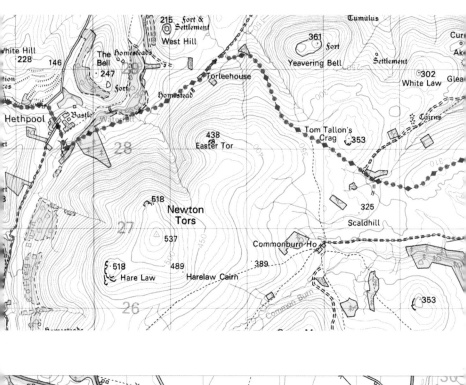

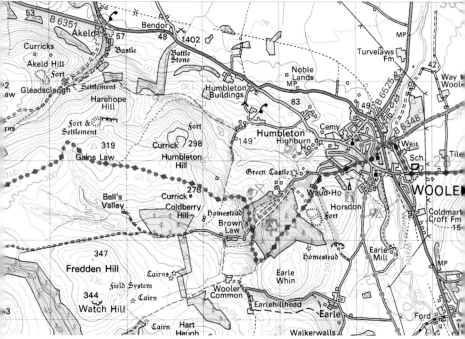

6
HETHPOOL TO WOOLER

SUMMARY

Distance: 13 km (8 miles).

Height Range: 80-340m.

Accommodation: B&B in Hethpool, hotels and B&Bs in Wooler. Youth Hostel and campsite in Wooler.

Food and Drink: Only available in Wooler.

Public Transport: Regular bus services Wooler to Berwick and Wooler to Alnwick.

Terrain Summary: A mainly level walk in the College Valley before a short steep climb into the northern Cheviot Hills. A high-level walk with excellent views follows before the route drops down to the Wooler Common Ponds. A final climb through woodland leads to a gradual descent into Wooler.

Opposite the cottages, go through the gate and follow the track to a bridge over the College Burn. Immediately after crossing the bridge, go left through the gorse to join a wide track leading into a wood. The three summits ahead of you are Harelaw (518m), Wester Tor (537m) and Easter Tor (438m).

After passing through the wood, follow the clear path to a fence and stile. At a junction beyond the stile, the path to the left leads down for 200m to the waterfalls of Hethpool Linn, a worthwhile detour and a lovely spot for a break if you need one. St Cuthbert's Way takes the right fork down over a burn and then climbs to cross a stile and continue over open ground towards a walled sheepfold. This is on the site of a prehistoric settlement, some of the stones of which were used in its construction. Join the track straight ahead. If you keep a sharp lookout, you may see feral goats on the slopes of Easter Tor and Yeavering Bell. They have been here for centuries.

The track crosses a small wood and becomes a gravel road which leads towards the buildings of Torleehouse. St Cuthbert's Way skirts the property to its right before rejoining the gravel road. Immediately before a gate, turn

Feral goat near Yeavering Bell.

right to follow a clear track steeply uphill towards a gate
and ladder stile on the far left.

Yeavering Bell, to the left of the path, is Northumberland's largest hillfort, covering an area of over 5 hectares
(13 acres), surrounded by a rubble wall 1km long. Within
the wall the outlines of no fewer than 130 hut circles have
been found. The fort is believed to have been one of the
tribal strongholds of the Votadini, the people inhabiting
Northumberland and the Lothians in Roman times.

At the foot of Yeavering Bell, on its northern side,
is the site of the Anglian palace of Ad Gefrin, where St
Paulinus, at the invitation of the Christian King Edwin,
is said to have baptised 3,000 Northumbrians in the
nearby River Glen in 627AD – not too many years before
St Cuthbert came to the area. The site of Ad Gefrin was
excavated between 1953 and 1962 and revealed a series
of great halls built of timber, an open air meeting-place
with tiered seating and a small church which appears

to have replaced a pagan temple, next to a Christian cemetery. There is a memorial plaque to Ad Gefrin on the Kirknewton to Wooler road. In 2006 the land was bought by the Ad Gefrin Trust and an interpretive trail created around the site.

Continue to climb steadily over a cross-track and carry on for a further kilometre. Leave the track by a cairn, forking left onto a path leading towards the prominent rocks of Tom Tallon's Crag. Keep well below the crag and to its right to reach a wall with a gate and ladder stile. This wall was built in 1859 using the stones of a Bronze Age cairn known as Tom Tallon's Grave which formerly stood here. It provided enough stone to build a wall 1km long and 1.5m high.

Waymark by Yeavering Bell.

View near Tom Tallon's Crag.

Note: *The section between the cairn and Wooler can be arduous in very bad weather conditions such as heavy snow or thick mist. An alternative route if you are unsure of proceeding is not to turn left at the cairn but to stay on the main track. It leads eventually to Commonburn House. From there, a private tarred road leads into Wooler, picking up the route of St Cuthbert's Way again at the Forest Enterprise car park on Wooler Common.*

Descend from the wall to join a gravel track coming in from the left, and cross a burn. Leave the track by a footpath on the left, climbing towards a gate in a wall. Do not go through this gate but turn left to follow the path beside the wall. Go through a gate and after a further 100m, a third gate takes the path through the wall to join a track. When the wall turns sharply left, leave the wall and follow the track that bears left at an angle to join a track around the head of a valley. This is part of an area of meltwater channels known as the Trows, gouged out by the water formed beneath the ice 10,000 years ago when the Cheviot Icefield melted.

On reaching a wall, the track bears right above the valley and leads below the summit of Gains Law (319m), revealing a panoramic view of the Cheviot range. From left to right are the shapely summit of Hedgehope (714m), the great whaleback of Cheviot itself (815m), the rocky peak of The Schil (601m), the Newton Tors (518m) and the now-familiar Yeavering Bell (361m). Far to your left on a clear day the summit of Ros Castle (315m), highest point of the northern Fell Sandstone ridge, can be seen across the valley of the Till.

Continue downhill through a gate to a junction. Take the right fork. To the left is Humbleton Hill, crowned by a hillfort with a spectacular ravine below it which is also a meltwater channel. Further north, the view extends over the Milfield Plain to the Fell Sandstone ridges of Broomridge and Doddington Moor. In early prehistoric times, the plain was a vast lake, which eventually drained away through the Till and the Tweed. In the Bronze Age the plain became an important centre of population. Crop marks and excavation have revealed the sites of a series of wooden henge monuments connected by an avenue.

The northern slopes of Humbleton Hill were the site of the Battle of Homildon in 1402. Shakespeare's *Henry IV Part I* opens with news of the battle, fought between the English led by Henry Percy (better known as Harry Hotspur) and the Scots led by Archibald, Earl of Douglas. The Scots army, laden with plunder after a raid into Northumberland, found Hotspur blocking their route to the Tweed and were forced to make a stand on Humbleton Hill. The battle was won by the English, with heavy losses inflicted on the Scots by the English archers. Douglas himself lost an eye and was taken prisoner.

A level walk across Coldberry Hill follows before you drop down to another track. Turn left onto this, go through a gate, then turn immediately right through another gate onto a clear track leading to a wicket gate into a wood. Drop steeply down through the wood to a gravel path in the valley of the Humbleton Burn. Turn right to a car park with information board. This path alongside the burn forms part of a Nature Trail laid out by Forest Enterprise. If you had turned left, you would soon have reached two ponds created as a haven for wildlife and also to provide an emergency water supply for Forest Enterprise.

Cross the road to join the bridleway opposite, walking alongside the burn to a gate. Follow the track uphill, and bear left at a fork in the track to a cross-track running along a wall. This is a bridleway from Wooler Common Farm (on the right) leading into Wooler. Beyond the wall is the valley of Earle Dene, which forms a gorge between the slopes of Earle Whin and Earle Hill.

Join the track going left to a gate leading into the forest, and walk through the forest on a clear track. The first side track to the left leads to a picnic table with a fine view back over the Cheviots. On leaving the forest, follow the track downhill. The ramparts to your right are those of the Kettles Hillfort. Beyond this is a valley in which can be found the Pin Well, so called because local people once used to throw in bent pins on Fair Days to make a wish, particularly young ladies looking for a good husband!

The track leads down to a boggy area, home to two species of newt, and turns left to a gate by the white-painted Waud House. Go through the gate and down the track to Common Road and turn right. It becomes Ramseys Lane leading to Wooler Market Place. For the

Wooler.

youth hostel, turn right after 300m along a bridleway (signposted). For Highburn House campsite, turn left opposite the bridleway into Broomey Road which leads to a path down to the campsite.

WOOLER

Wooler is the largest settlement in the Cheviot Hills area, with a population of about 1,800. Founded in the 12th century as one of the baronies into which Northumberland was divided by the Normans, it was held by the de Muschamp family who erected a castle, originally on the outskirts of the town, at a site close to the Humbleton Burn known today as 'Green Castle', and later on the mound behind the church, known locally as the 'Tory', where a few fragments of wall still remain.

Wooler has been a market town since the 13th century, and today still has one of the most important livestock markets in north-east England, with weekly sales held at the Mart on Berwick Road. It was the importance of the livestock market which brought the railway to Wooler in 1887, when the Cornhill branch of the North-Eastern Railway was opened, linking the town with the main line at Alnmouth. Passenger services only operated until 1930, although freight traffic lasted until 1948, when severe floods washed away the bridge at Ilderton, 5km south of Wooler.

Not unnaturally, the town endured frequent and often severe raids by marauding Scots over a 300-year period between the 14th and 16th centuries, and later suffered two disastrous fires, which accounts for the lack of pre-Victorian buildings. In Georgian and Victorian times, Wooler gained a reputation as a health resort, notable visitors including Sir Walter Scott and Grace Darling.

In the 19th century, Wooler became the seat of the Glendale District Council which covered a large and sparsely populated area of north Northumberland. At the local government reorganisation in 1974, Glendale became part of the Borough of Berwick-upon-Tweed, but Wooler remains the focal point for the Glendale and Cheviot area, with a wide range of shops, services and accommodation to cater for the local population and a growing number of visitors.

7
WOOLER TO FENWICK

SUMMARY

Distance: 19km (11.5 miles).

Height Range: 55–175 m.

Accommodation: Hotels and B&Bs in Wooler, B&B in Fenwick, hotel and B&Bs in both Lowick and Beal-West Mains (5km and 2km from Fenwick respectively).

Food and Drink: Only available in Wooler and Beal-West Mains.

Public Transport: Regular buses from Wooler to Alnwick and Wooler to Berwick and from Fenwick (on the A1) to Alnwick and Berwick.

Terrain Summary: An easy section with no steep hills to climb. Some road walking on quiet country roads. Despite the lack of altitude, there are excellent views throughout the walk.

To resume the route, go down Church Street from the Market Place, passing St Mary's Church. There has been a church on this site since the 12th century. The present building dates from 1765 but has undergone extensive restoration in more recent years. Opposite the Police Station, steps lead up to the War Memorial on the site of Wooler's castle, of which only fragments remain. Continue down Church Street to cross the A697 and the iron bridge opposite. Turn right past the bowling club, alongside Scott's Park and the Wooler Water, following the course of the dismantled Alnwick-Cornhill railway line, into Brewery Road.

Turn left to pass Glendale Middle School. The school is on the site of a World War Two prison camp, and the lions on the school gateposts were made by Italian prisoners of war. Continue uphill along the road as far as the sharp bend at the top, then go straight ahead up a track between hedges to a gate out onto Weetwood Bank. Follow the path ahead, which bears right, up the bank. After 300m take the left fork. It becomes a clear track across

Weetwood Moor aiming towards the left-hand one of two plantations. Shortly before the wood is reached, a tumbledown wall is seen. Continue along the right-hand side of this wall towards two adjacent gates.

WEETWOOD MOOR

Weetwood Moor forms part of the Fell Sandstone moorland which lies between the Cheviot Hills and the coastal plain. It is rich in prehistoric remains. If time permits, a detour of 1.2km takes you to some fine examples of cup-and-ring marked rocks. To reach them, take the *right-hand* track at the fork and follow this cairned track across the moor to a gate and stile at the right-hand corner of a belt of woodland. Cross the stile and look for a cairn on the low rock outcrops to your left which indicates the position of the main group of rock carvings. There are more examples on other rocks in the vicinity. Return to St Cuthbert's Way by the same track.

The moor is also known locally as Whitsun Bank, as it was the site of the 'Whitsun Tryst', a great annual fair for cattle, horses and sheep held on the third Monday in May until the late 19th century. There are many tales associated with the fair. One tells of a raiding party led by the Kers of Cessford, who had lain in wait at the foot of Humbleton Hill to ambush a party of Storeys, their sworn enemies, who were on their way to the fair. However, the Storeys were tipped off about the ambush and escaped. Ker and his men then made their way to the fair themselves – much to the consternation of the local people – but they merely joined in the fun.

Another tale relates to Sir Walter Scott's grandfather, who attended the fair to buy a small flock of sheep with £30 of his shepherd's money – a considerable sum in those days. Seeing a horse that took his fancy, he bought the animal instead of the sheep. Within a few days he had resold the horse for double the price and used the money to buy a sizeable flock of sheep – an excellent example of horse-trading!

Go through the right-hand gate and keep to the left edge of the field, passing two small adjacent woods on your left, until you reach another gate on the left by a wood.

Weetwood Bridge.

Go through this gate and bear right from the end of the wood to a stile in the field corner. Cross the stile, turn left and follow the track, with a plantation on your left, to a gate with a fine view of the Till Valley and the hump-backed Weetwood Bridge. The River Till, the only English tributary of the Tweed, starts its life as the River Breamish high on the slopes of Cheviot. Follow a path down the hillside towards the bridge. Climb the stile, cross the road with care and walk over the bridge.

The bridge dates from the 16th century and was restored 200 years later. It has recently undergone major renovation which will secure its future. The work was undertaken by the Northumberland County Council's Highways Department and the bridge has now been taken off the national 'Buildings at Risk' register. Its predecessor was used by the English Army under the command of the Earl of Surrey on their way to victory at the Battle of Flodden in 1513.

The Duke of Suffolk, another of the 16th century English commanders, said at the time, "We shall give them such a buffet upon their Borders as shall make them to repent it, seeing that the corn now in the houses and stacks the which they should live by, for the whole year, shall be so destroyed that they shall be the more easier to meddle with hereafter". Despite these tough words, the Scots were always fearsome opponents in a fight.

Follow the road, bearing right around the grounds of 18th century Weetwood Hall. Ahead is Doddington Moor, where local legend says St Cuthbert tended sheep as a child. A small cave here is known as Cuddy's Cave, Cuddy being an affectionate form of Cuthbert. There are two iron age hillforts on the moor, more cup-and-ring marked rocks and the remains of a stone circle, showing that this was an important centre in far distant times. Doddington Quarry produces the attractive pink sandstone of which the older buildings in Wooler High Street and many of the village houses and farmhouses have been built.

The road leads to the farms of East and West Horton. On the way it passes over the course of the main gas

The track from Horton.

supply line taking natural gas from the Frigg Field in the North Sea to the south to heat homes and offices. West Horton is the site of an important Borders stronghold – Horton Castle, first mentioned in 1415. In 1542 a report from the Border Commissioners stated, "At Horton there is a greatte towne with a Barmekyn of Sir Roger Greyes inheritaunce and his chief house in great decays for lack of contynuall reparations and great pitye yt were that yt should be suffered to decaye for yt standeth in a very convenient place for the defence of the country thereabouts". On 18th century maps, the castle is shown as a ruin, and a print of 1728 shows it in a ruinous state with vegetation growing from all the walls. It is believed that the castle was subsequently used as a source of stone to build the farmhouses of East and West Horton.

At a T-junction, turn left. This road from Horton to Lowick follows the course of the 'Devil's Causeway', a Roman Road which linked Corbridge with Tweedmouth. The Devil's Causeway is shown on old maps running dead straight, north to south, for many miles, but most of it has now disappeared.

Follow its course for just 300m and then turn right along a metalled track. The track goes over a slight rise and then drops down through a gate. Bear left with the main track to cross the Hetton Burn. Continue going left and right with the track to a road with the former Hazelrigg School on the right. Continue straight ahead along the road for about 800m until you reach a wood on the left, just past a lane on the right which goes to Old Hazelrigg.

Take the track on the left immediately beyond the wood, passing an abandoned quarry but then leaving the clear track through a gate on the right into a field – watch carefully for the marker here as the turn can be missed if you are not looking out for it. Follow the left edge of the field through two gates to a broad cross-track. Turn right towards the trees on the skyline.

On reaching the wood, go left through a gate onto a clear track and through another gate into St Cuthbert's Cave Wood, which is owned and managed by the National Trust. Near the far end of the wood, a clear path on the right leads to St Cuthbert's Cave, a dramatic sandstone overhang where the saint's body is said to

St Cuthbert's Cave.

have been taken by the monks in 875AD during their flight from Lindisfarne following repeated Viking raids on the island.

The cave is a wonderfully evocative place and you can imagine the monks laying down their precious burden to shelter there after the traumatic events of the preceding days. St Cuthbert's body was carried around northern England for eight years in all, eventually finding a home at Chester-le-Street. It was enshrined there for more than a century before reaching its final resting-place in the then newly-built Durham Cathedral in 995AD.

After viewing the cave, return to the main track and turn right to a gate. Turn right again and walk uphill to a gate on the saddle between Greensheen Hill and Cockenheugh. From here you get your first sight of your destination – Holy Island, with Lindisfarne Castle prominent on its crag. Walk downhill through the gate on the left and follow the bridleway, aiming for the double gates seen below, which enable you to cross Middleton Burn by a footbridge. Climb towards the gorse-covered cliffs on the skyline and keep left of them to reach a gate out onto a clear track. Go right, off the route for about 50m, to get a superb view of the coast with Holy Island, Lindisfarne Castle, Budle Bay, Bamburgh Castle and the Farne Islands clearly seen on a good day. The woods immediately below you, around Greymare Farm, are known as the Grey Mare's Tail, from their shape.

Return to the route where St Cuthbert's Way is joined by two more long-distance footpaths opened in 2006 — the Northumberland Coast Path, a 103km trail from Cresswell to Berwick-upon-Tweed, part of the North Sea Trail, a European project offering over 5000km of coastal trails around the North Sea Basin, and St Oswald's Way, which links Lindisfarne with Heavenfield (near Hexham). Continue towards the wood ahead, ignoring tracks to the left, which lead to peat workings. On entering the wood, take the forestry track to the right and keep left at the first junction, following the track until it bears right. Follow the footpath straight ahead. Ignore a path going off to the left then cross a broad track and continue straight ahead crossing a number of bridged ditches to reach a gate and stile leading out of the wood

The track ahead, known as Dolly Gibson's Lonnen, is an ancient 'green road' and follows the edge of the wood.

Holy Island from Fawcet Hill.

It can be muddy after rain. Continue on and when the wood edge bends left, keep on the track leading straight ahead along the field edge.

The woodland here is known as Kyloe Old Wood, and it was here that some of the original *Leylandii* cypress stock was raised in the 19th century, when the woods were owned by the Leyland family of nearby Haggerston Castle. It has since become one of the most popular (and most controversial) hedging plants in the country. Alongside his interest in silviculture, Christopher John Leyland's first love was the sea. He joined the Royal Navy at the age of 13 and served the colours for ten years. When he was 40 he inherited the Haggerston Estate and invested in the world's first steam turbine-powered vessel, the *Turbinia* (now on permanent exhibition at Newcastle's Discovery Museum). It created a sensation at the 1897 Spithead Review, steaming through the fleet at an amazing 34 knots. Leyland skippered the *Turbinia* on its epic voyage to the 1900 Paris Exhibition.

At the corner of the field, the track bears left and continues to a road at Blawearie Cottage. Turn right and follow the road downhill into Fenwick. This minor road was once the Great North Road until the current route taken by the A1 replaced it in the 19th century.

There are no facilities in Fenwick apart from a B&B. The nearest facilities are at the Beal crossroads on the A1, 2km north of the village, where the Lindisfarne Inn, B&Bs and a garage with shop are to be found. To reach Beal, we recommend using the minor road at the west end of Fenwick (unsignposted) which passes Mount Hooley to reach the A1 almost opposite the garage.

ISLANDSHIRE

When St Cuthbert's Way leaves Shiellow Wood to follow the track known as Dolly Gibson's Lonnen along the edge of Buckton Moor, you enter the ancient district known as Islandshire. Until 1844 it formed part of the County Palatine of Durham, but was then incorporated for the first time into Northumberland. The name has survived through successive local government reorganisations

Shiellow Wood.

– initially as the Norham and Islandshire Rural District, then as the Islandshire Ward of the Borough of Berwick-upon-Tweed and most recently as the Islandshire Ward of the Northumberland County Council.

The coastal area of Islandshire provided the monks of the Anglo-Saxon monastery and the later medieval Priory of Lindisfarne with their daily needs, as this ancient rhyme makes plain:

> *From Goswick we've geese, from Cheswick we've cheese*
> *From Buckton we've venison in store*
> *From Swinhoe we've bacon, but the Scots have it taken*
> *And the Prior is longing for more.*

The name Beal comes from Bee-hill, the provider of honey to Lindisfarne in earlier times.

Dolly Gibson's Lonnen and the onward track from Fenwick Granary to the coast, known as 'Fishers Back Row', are certainly of ancient origin, having supposedly been used by the monks of Lindisfarne to transport peat which they had dug from their workings at Holburn Moss on the far side of Shiellow Wood.

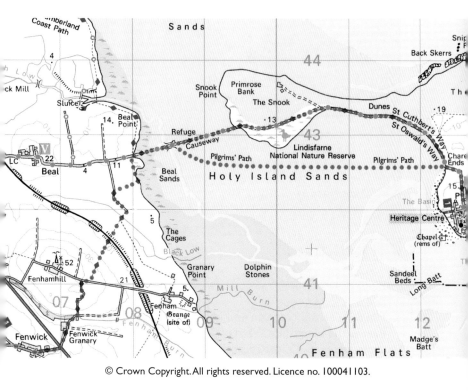

8
FENWICK TO LINDISFARNE

SUMMARY

Distance: 10km (6 miles) using the causeway road or 8km (5 miles) using the Pilgrims' Path across the sands.

Height Range: Sea level to 40m.

Accommodation: B&B in Fenwick, hotels and B&Bs off-route in Lowick and Beal, West Mains. On Lindisfarne there are hotels and B&Bs but advance booking is strongly recommended. CAMPING IS STRICTLY PROHIBITED ON THE ISLAND. Campsite at Goswick (3.5km north of the causeway).

Food and Drink: Café at Beal Farm (1km from the causeway), cafes and restaurants on Lindisfarne.

Public Transport: Regular buses along the A1 between Berwick and Alnwick pass Fenwick and Beal, West Mains. Irregular bus service Lindisfarne to Berwick. Holy Island Minibus Service can offer journeys to A1 at Beal or Berwick for small parties.

Terrain Summary: Clear tracks lead to the causeway where you can choose to follow the road or the path over the sands to reach the end of the Way on Lindisfarne (Holy Island).

At the T-junction in Fenwick, turn right through the village to the A1. **Take extreme care crossing this very busy major road to the lane opposite.** To get a better sight-line, the recommended crossing point is by the bus shelter. As you look to your right, you will see a group of trees on a hill to the left-hand side of the road. This is known as Grizel's Clump.

In 1685, the 19-year-old Grizel Cochrane, dressed as a man, held up the mail coach from London here, and seized the death warrant of her father Sir John Cochrane, who had been sentenced for his part in the Earl of Argyll's insurrection. The delay brave Grizel caused gave her father time to obtain a royal pardon from King James II.

The crossing on the East Coast Main Line.

She later married John Ker of Morriston, near Earlston in Lauderdale, and is buried at Legerwood, where her tombstone records that she died on 21 March 1748 aged 82.

Follow the lane past the buildings of Fenwick Granary, noting the dovecot among the outbuildings. The lane bends right then crosses a burn. After passing cottages on your right, join a path on the left leading uphill towards an abandoned wooded quarry. Follow the path around the quarry and up to a road.

Turn right along the road and take a path on the left leading downhill to the railway line. This is the East Coast Main Line where trains reach speeds of up to 125mph. **Please exercise extreme caution when crossing the line.** You must use the telephone provided to contact the signalman to receive permission to cross the line in safety. You will also be required to use the telephone on the other side of the line to inform the signalman that you have crossed.

Should you be concerned about crossing the railway (it can be difficult for groups), an alternative permissive route is available. Instead of turning left onto the path, as above, continue with the road for 800m to cross the railway by a bridge. Turn left onto a gravel track which is followed alongside the railway until you reach the ladder stile on the direct path.

Go straight ahead across the field to a gate and bridge over the Beal Cast burn. Bear left across the next field to a gate. Join a broad farm track and, when the track bears slightly left, turn right along a clear path across fields to a gate which leads onto the foreshore of Beal Sands. Turn left and walk along between two lines of concrete blocks, part of the World War Two coastal defences, to reach the Causeway Road to Holy Island. In the car park here safe crossing times are displayed, together with interpretation panels on the Lindisfarne National Nature Reserve.

If you have planned your day in advance, it should be safe for you to follow the causeway road onto the island. The road takes the shortest route to the island, crossing the bridge over South Low, then over the sands

On the Pilgrims' Path.

to the Snook, the western end of the island. It then keeps
to the edge of the dunes to Chare Ends, the entrance to
Holy Island village. The old Pilgrims' Route, marked by
a line of poles, crosses the sands directly from the bridge
to Chare Ends.

SAFE CROSSING TIMES

Having noted the safe crossing times for the day, you will
need to plan accordingly. If you have not secured accommodation on the island, you will need to ensure that there
is sufficient time for you to walk off as well as onto the
island and, of course, allow good time for exploration.
Examples from a crossing timetable are shown below:

Example A: safe times from 10.02am to 5.05pm, and from
10.05pm to 5.30am

Example B: safe times from 4.30am to 12.05pm, and from
5.05pm to 12.30am

If you are crossing on a day with a similar pattern to (A)
you must get over and back between 10am and 5pm,
otherwise you will be stranded on the island until after
10pm. If the crossing pattern is as (B) you can cross at any
time up to midday and stay until after 5pm, when you
can safely return any time up to midnight.

If you intend to use the Pilgrims' Path across the sands
to reach or return from the island, be aware that the sands
are covered by water for a much longer period than the
causeway. You should aim to cross only during the middle of the safe period to avoid deep water on the route.
If you can, you should cross barefoot or in wellingtons,
as water remains on the sands even at low tide. Join the
Pilgrim's Route after crossing the bridge after South Low,
taking a line from the refuge box along the line of posts
to Chare Ends, a distance of 3.7km (2.3 miles).

We do recommend that walkers try to use the Pilgrims'
Route to end the walk, as it is a wonderful experience
crossing the sands to Lindisfarne this way. It is however
quite slow going, so please allow a good two hours for
the crossing.

HOLY ISLAND

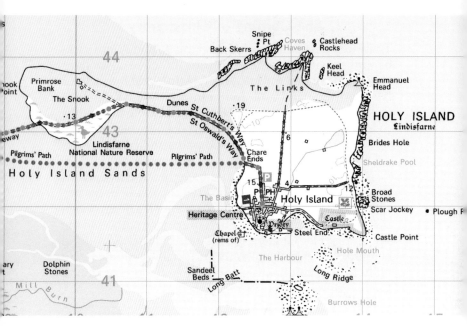

Holy Island, also known as Lindisfarne, is one of Western Europe's most famous Christian sites. It was here that St Aidan founded a monastery in 635AD, and thus established a base from where the Christian message was sent out across the then pagan north of England. Although it is with the high achievements of this period that Holy Island is most closely associated, the island has a wealth of sites and features which relate to all periods of an eventful history.

Human occupation of what is now Holy Island began long before the era of St Aidan when the island was still attached to the mainland. During this time, several thousand years before Christ, Holy Island was a low, wooded hill facing the sea which appears to have been a rich area for hunting and fishing. Discoveries from this period include large sites used for the manufacture of flint artefacts.

The clearance of the natural woodland on Holy Island was accomplished about 5,000 years ago when hunting was replaced by settled agriculture as a means of subsistence. Evidence of a later Roman presence exists only in pottery fragments which may have come from a trading ship wrecked off this treacherous coastline.

The Coming of Christianity

The spread of Christianity from Holy Island is inextricably linked with St Cuthbert. During an active missionary career, St Cuthbert travelled from Holy Island throughout Northern England and Southern Scotland. Walking St Cuthbert's Way today provides an insight into the lengths of journey he would have undertaken on his missions – and he did not have the good paths and tracks, or the convenient accommodation, that we have today.

The stories of his deeds and piety became legendary, the more so following the reported discovery of his miraculously preserved body 11 years after his death, when his coffin was opened. The 7th century also witnessed the flowering of the Golden Age of Northumbria, the cultural accomplishments of which are principally associated with Holy Island, culminating of course in the production of the magnificent Lindisfarne Gospels.

St Cuthbert of Farne on Holy Island.

St Cuthbert's Isle.

Yet, as the seeds of the Golden Age of Northumbria were sown and nurtured on Holy Island, so the island also saw the beginning of the destruction of its achievements.

Viking Raids

In 793AD the first recorded Viking raid on Britain took place on Holy Island, heralding a long period of violent incursions which led to the conquest of Northern England. We can scarcely imagine the terror that must have been felt by the peaceful and God-fearing community when the longships came out of the east with war, pillage and destruction as their aims.

The raids continued with increasing frequency, and in 875AD the monks had to flee the monastery, taking with them the venerated body of St Cuthbert, and other treasures including the precious Gospels.

Lindisfarne Priory

St Cuthbert's name and life inspired the building of Lindisfarne Priory, which began about 1120. This elaborate structure, the remains of which are now conserved and managed by English Heritage, was designed to provide a suitable setting for the grave of Northumbria's most venerated saint. The Priory was however to suffer frequent attacks during the Border Wars with Scotland

Lindisfarne Castle from the slipway.

which commenced at the end of the 13th century and continued, on and off, for 300 years.

During this period, the Priory was fortified and provided a safe refuge when raids (by either side) were in progress. The Priory was, like so many buildings of its kind, to fall victim not to the Scots but to the policies of Henry VIII when he ordered the dissolution of the monasteries and the destruction of their treasures.

The Castle

Henry VIII however ordered the construction of the island's most imposing landmark, Lindisfarne Castle. Holy Island held great strategic importance during these troubled times, providing a vital base for organising war efforts against the Scots. The castle was also to have a significant role in the English Civil War when the Parliamentary garrison held out against a long Royalist siege.

A rather less heroic episode in the castle's history was its short-lived seizure on behalf of the Jacobite cause by two members of the local Errington family in 1715. Following this incident, the castle suffered a long period of decay, from which it was finally rescued in 1902. In that year, the castle was purchased by Edward Hudson, founder of *Country Life* magazine, who commissioned the

Opposite: The Priory, Holy Island.

famous architect Edwin Lutyens to undertake a complete restoration programme.

Lutyens retained the outward appearance of the castle but transformed its interior into a stately, elegant retreat. The castle is now owned by the National Trust, who carefully conserve it as it was restored by Lutyens. It is open to the public.

On the opposite side of the harbour to the castle are the remains of a 17th century fort, which appears to have been constructed as a defence against Dutch privateers. Much of this structure has been lost to erosion by the sea, but the still striking remains have been protected through works directed by the Northumberland Coast Project and the county's archaeology service.

Island Life and Industries

The more recent history of Holy Island has left a legacy of remains relating to lost activities and industries. During the 19th century, a huge demand existed in northern England and Scotland for the supply of burnt lime, which was used to improve the fertility of previously unproductive soils. The soft limestones which are exposed in the north of the island provided an ideal raw material for this industry.

Lime kilns were built along the north of the island and a network of tramways was established between quarries,

Visitors on Holy Island.

kilns and jetties on the west. Impressive remains of this now extinct industry can be seen in the system of wide tracks which traverse the island, and in the substantial block of kilns at Castle Point, now owned by the National Trust.

Until the last century, fishing was also a mainstay for the economy of the island. In the mid-19th century about 50% of the island population of over 900 were engaged in herring fishing. The decline of the herring shoals – the 'silver darlings' of song and story – and the introduction of new fishing methods destroyed this industry by the time of the First World War. Reminders of this past way of life exist today in the three-storey herring houses near the harbour and in the black upturned hulks of the former sail-powered fishing boats which still line the harbour edge.

Today, Holy Island has a thriving community which is proud of its long history and traditions. Agriculture is still important, and during the summer months in particular the island is a focus for tourism, receiving many thousands of visitors from all over the world.

In recent years two new visitor attractions have opened, both located on Marygate in the village centre. The first is the Lindisfarne Heritage Centre which serves as an information centre for the island and has both permanent and temporary exhibitions. Its interactive 'Turning the Pages' computer screens enable the visitor to view individual pages of the Lindisfarne Gospels. Almost opposite the Heritage Centre is the Gospel Garden, recreated from a design that won a silver award at the Chelsea Flower Show in 2003.

Two further items that may be of interest to St Cuthbert's Way walkers are the 'St Cuthbert's Seat' that has been placed in the grounds of St Cuthbert's United Reform Church (to the left at the end of Marygate) and, in the Priory grounds, the bronze sculpture 'Cuthbert of Farne' by Fenwick Lawson, which was commissioned in 1999.

In the winter the island is a quieter place as far as visitors are concerned, but the ever-restless sea and the variable winds ensure that life at the sea edge is never dull. Although much has changed since St Cuthbert's time, he would still feel at home with the rocks, the sand, the tide and the seabirds if he were to return today.

St Cuthbert's Seat by the United Reform Church.

The Lindisfarne National Nature Reserve

The National Nature Reserve extends from Budle Bay in the south to Cheswick in the north. It covers 3,500 hectares of coastal habitat, mainly sand and mudflats, saltmarsh and dune. In autumn and winter the reserve provides food for up to 50,000 waders and wildfowl which arrive here from Arctic regions.

The dunes are also botanically rich, and because of its international importance for nature conservation, the whole reserve has been declared a Ramsar site (a wetland of major international importance), and a European Special Protection Area as well as a Site of Special Scientific Interest.

Six species of bird occurring here are internationally significant, the most important being the pale-bellied brent goose, of which there are fewer than 4,000 in the world. Most of these birds spend the winter on the reserve, along with up to 20,000 wigeon, a duck hunted by wildfowlers under permit, both species feeding on the *Zostera* or eel-grass which grows on the mudflats.

These areas, apparently lifeless to the casual observer, are in fact home to millions of marine animals such as lugworms and small snails (*Hydrobia*), and these provide the essential food for wading birds. Three species, the redshank, grey plover and bar-tailed godwit, reach internationally important numbers at Lindisfarne with a further ten species of birds of national significance, including the eider duck with its distinctive call, and the little dunlin.

Please try to limit disturbance to these sensitive species by keeping to the road to Holy Island during the winter months. Close views can be had from the causeway of some of the birds, especially as the tide ebbs.

As you reach the island proper, you will be aware of the extensive dune system to the north of the road. This has evolved over hundreds of years and is still in a state of flux. The hillier yellow dunes are dominated by marram grass, which relies on mobile sand to survive. Long root formations may be seen extending down through the exposed sections of dune.

Another plant of these foredunes is an introduction from New Zealand, the pirri-pirri bur. Although its carpets of bright green leaves appear relatively harmless, from July to October the burs develop. These disintegrate on contact and are a nightmare for walkers and wildlife alike. The plant is either an escapee from the castle garden or a throwback to the wool industry on the Tweed.

In the summer months, the dune flora is at its best with displays of orchids such as the northern marsh and marsh helleborine. Although the rabbit population is at times rather too healthy, these browsing animals do help to maintain the short turf upon which the diversity of dune plants depends. At times when rabbit numbers are insufficient to manage the vegetation, cattle and mechanical methods are employed. The dark green fritillary and grayling butterflies may also be seen on the wing on warmer days.

If you would like to explore further the natural delights of the nature reserve, a self-guided walk leaflet is available from the Heritage Centre, the reserve bird hides or the main car park on Holy Island.

Holy Island text supplied by the Countryside Service of Northumberland County Council. Nature Reserve notes provided by Phil Davey of Natural England's Northumbria Team.

WALKING FROM LINDISFARNE TO MELROSE

This chapter provides the directions for anyone walking east to west. The background and historical material can be referred to in the main text.

Lindisfarne to Wooler

From the mainland end of the causeway, turn left and walk along the shore past the concrete blocks. After 300m turn inland through a gate and follow the path across the field to a broad track, turn left and then pass through a gate on the right. Walk diagonally over the field, cross the Beal Cast burn and continue to the railway line ahead. You must use the telephone provided to contact the signalman to obtain permission to cross the line and report your safe crossing using the telephone on the other side. Climb up the field edge path to reach a road. Turn right onto it and continue for 100m, then turn left onto a track which goes round a double bend and descends to another road. Turn right to pass Fenwick Granary and reach the A1. **Please cross this busy road with extreme care.** We recommend the point opposite the bus shelter as the best line of sight.

Walk up the road into Fenwick village and turn left up the hill past the village hall. Go over the brow and down over a crossroads to Blawearie cottage. Turn left opposite the cottage onto a path along the edge of the field. It bends right to reach the edge of the wood. Follow the path (here called Dolly Gibson's Lonnen) along the wood edge. Continue on a path alongside a plantation fence crossing a number of ditches. Continue ahead until you reach a forestry road.

Cross this road and continue ahead to join another forestry road. Carry on along this, ignoring all side tracks, until you reach a cross track. Turn left here to leave the wood. 600m after leaving the wood, the route turns right at a gate, but if you continue for about 50m you get a

Opposite: Waymark on Crookedshaws in the Yetholm to Harestanes section.

superb view of the coast taking in Holy Island, Bamburgh Castle and the Farne Islands.

Return to the gate and go through as directed to cross open land with crags on your left. Go downhill to the double gates at the crossing of Middleton Burn. Climb steadily, trending slightly left, and go through a gate. Turn right to another gate at the brow of the hill, and walk down the path beside the wood. Turn left into St Cuthbert's Cave Wood. To visit the Cave, take the clear path on the left about 200m into the wood, returning afterwards to the main path.

Continue along the path for 400m and turn right through a gate onto a clear track. After 500m, at the foot of the hill, turn left through the left-hand gate to follow a path along the field edges, through two gates, emerging at a gate onto a clear track by an old quarry. After 150m, at the edge of the wood, turn right onto a road. Walk down the road for a kilometre to a crossroads, and go straight ahead along the track.

The Cheviots from Weetwood Moor.

The track bends left and right and crosses the Hetton Burn, then climbs steadily along the field edges and through a gate to reach a metalled track. Follow this over Town Law to the road.

Turn left, and after 300m, in East Horton, turn right through West Horton. Continue following the road for nearly two kilometres and, after a sharp left turn, walk down to Weetwood Bridge. Cross the bridge and then, with care, cross the B6349 road. Cross the ladder stile and take the path going half-right up the slope to a gate.

Go through the gate, bearing half-right for 300m with a plantation on your right, then go right over a stile at a field corner. Cross the field and go through a gate at the right-hand edge of the wood and then turn right. Walk along the field edge to a gate onto the open moor, then cross Weetwood Moor on a clear path to a junction. Follow the path to the right downhill to a gate, then follow the track downhill to meet a road. Go straight ahead on the road and walk downhill past Glendale Middle School and Weetwood Avenue. Turn right onto a path alongside Scott's Park and the bowling club to a road, turn left over the bridge and cross the A697 into Church Street, which leads up to Wooler Market Place.

Wooler to Yetholm

Leave Wooler by Ramsey's Lane which, beyond Broomey Road, becomes Common Road. Turn left onto the bridleway opposite the last houses on your right to pass the white-painted Waud House. Through the gate, turn right, then left alongside the boggy area, bearing right onto a path going uphill leading to the forest.

Enter the forest by the stile at the left-hand gate and follow the clear track. Partway along, a side track on the right leads to a picnic table with a fine view towards the Cheviots. On leaving the forest, continue ahead for 200m and then turn sharp right to descend to the road by a car park and picnic area with a Forest Enterprise information board.

Cross the road and the car park and turn left to climb steeply up through the wood. Go through a wicket gate at the top of the wood and continue on the path for 300m, bearing round to the left. Turn left through a gate then right through another gate to follow the track across the north side of Coldberry Hill, with Humbleton Hill prominent to your right.

After another path joins from the right the track climbs to traverse under the summit of Gains Law (319m) then round the head of a small valley to head south-west across the moor. Bear left when the track splits and continue to a wall. Keep to the left of the wall until a gate takes you through to the north side. Go through two more gates, then bear right by a fourth gate to drop into the valley below.

Join a gravel track and turn right. Cross a burn then leave the track on a path climbing to reach a wall with a gate and ladder stile. Continue with the path, skirting below the rocks of Tom Tallon's Crag. Join a broader path at a cairn and turn right, then head steadily downhill for 1.5km, crossing a wall by a ladder stile. At the foot of the hill turn left onto a broad track passing Torleehouse.

When the track ends, continue ahead on the path, cross a burn by a footbridge and continue across open ground with the College Burn below to the right. Go through a wood and follow a wide track before turning right through gorse on a path to the bridge over the burn, and follow the track uphill to meet a road at Hethpool. Go straight ahead on the road and when it bends to the right, turn left through a gate and follow the farm road for 2km to Elsdonburn Farm.

View north from Gainslaw.`

Here go left, cross a bridge and turn right past the bungalow to follow a farm track bearing left to a ford. Cross the burn and go over the stile into the field to your right. Cross the field to a stile leading into the wood. Walk through the wood and leave it at another stile. Descend to cross Tuppies Sike Burn, then follow the path, climbing steadily over open ground to reach the Border fence with its twin signs saying 'Welcome to England' and 'Welcome to Scotland'.

Go through the gate and follow the signs half-left over a rise and then down across a boggy area, rising to meet the Pennine Way. Turn right and follow the clear track down to the road. Turn right and walk along the road for 1.5km into Kirk Yetholm.

Yetholm to Harestanes

From the green at Kirk Yetholm, follow the signs down the lane to the youth hostel. Walk past the hostel and go half-left along a track to a gate. Once through the gate, turn left and head for the bridge over the Bowmont Water.

Go up steps to the road, turn right across the bridge, and go left through a gate onto the haugh where there are often cattle grazing. Head to the right of the pylon and continue beside the fence. Pass through two sets of gates into the lane known as Back Dykes and continue along it to a minor road.

Turn right past the cemetery and turn left at the junction with the main road. Walk along the road for 600m and at the next junction, go left at Primsidemill. Follow the road for about 800m then turn right as signed, climbing up a disused farm track.

At the top of the rise, go left over a stile into the field. Climb up through the small clump of trees. Cross a stile in the fence straight ahead, turn right and cross another stile, then turn left continuing uphill and go through a small gate. Bear right here and follow the wall as it climbs over Crookedshaws Hill, descends briefly, then climbs again over Wideopen Hill, at 368m the highest point on the walk.

Follow the wall as it descends towards a crossing wall. Cross this by a ladder stile and descend towards the summit of Grubbit Law. Follow the path below the summit and descend, turning right at a path junction. On

Wideopen Hill, the highest point on the Way.

reaching a gate, go through it and walk down the wide grass verge. Cross a stile and turn left, following the field down above the small burn.

Near the foot of the field, bear sharp right to meet a track. Follow this track round a sharp left bend, then quite steeply downhill bearing right. Leave the track to walk across the field to the footbridge over the Kale Water. Cross the bridge and turn right along the road.

At the next road junction, turn left and follow this minor road over a rise, then down to a junction. Turn left and walk into Morebattle. Walk through the village and continue with the B6401 for a kilometre passing Cowbog Farm on the right. At the next junction turn left as signed and walk down this minor road, round several bends, for 2.5km to reach Cessford Castle.

Follow the road past the castle. At a small triangle of

grass, turn right and walk down past the telephone box at the cottages of Cessford. Go straight ahead up the clear track. Follow this track round a sharp left turn, then along field edges towards a wood. Turn right along the side of the wood to its end, turn left and then right alongside a wall to a step stile. Turn left and follow the walls around the field edge to enter a wood through a gate. Keep close to the wood's edge until the path drops down to cross a burn, then climbs steeply to leave the wood. The path then turns right and follows the field edges to climb up towards the buildings of Brownrigg.

At the road turn left then right towards woodland. Turn into the wood and follow the clear path to a road. Turn right downhill to the buildings of Littledeanlees. Go through the wicket gate into the field with the cottage to your right. At a fence turn left downhill, veering left by a wood to a waymark. Go downhill and through a gate down to a footbridge over the Oxnam Water, and then climb up the track to a road and follow it straight ahead towards a wood. Turn left into the wood and follow the path through the wood to reach Dere Street. This Roman road is followed for about 800m to Jedfoot. When the track ends, go right on the road and immediately left. Cross the Jed Water by the road bridge, then cross the road with care and follow steps down to walk along by the Jed Water. Turn left along the Teviot when the two rivers meet.

After 800m, turn right over the graceful suspension bridge, then right again. Follow the signs, turning left to walk along a field edge and continuing through the Monteviot House estate. Harestanes Visitor Centre is a short diversion and is clearly signposted.

Harestanes to Melrose

To regain the route from Harestanes, follow any of the signed walk routes or Dere Street signs. Pick up St Cuthbert's Way again and turn left to follow it across the minor road and up through the estate woodland to another road. Cross this road and go over a stile into a large field.

Follow the field edges until the route becomes fenced on both sides. Follow the path as it winds through the trees up to Lilliardsedge. Lady Lilliard's Stone is a short diversion here over a stile to the left.

Continue with the path through the trees, across open fields and then through more woodland. At a minor road turn right and walk along the road for a kilometre to the village of Maxton. Turn right in Maxton and then left for Maxton Kirk. At the car park, keep ahead and then left past the kirk. At the end of the enclosure, turn right and follow the path down a long flight of steps.

The path continues beside the Tweed, rising and falling through the woods with several flights of steps, but is always clearly signposted. Swing right with the river. Eventually you emerge onto open ground and walk along through a field to Mertoun Bridge. Go up steps, cross the road with care and go down steps on the other side to regain the riverside path.

Continue with the path round a big left-hand bend of the river to reach St Boswells Golf Club. Follow the path next to the golf course, keeping to the bank beside the fence, then continuing alongside the fence to a lane. Turn left up the lane past the clubhouse, then turn right and first left down Braeheads Road. Turn right to walk through St Boswells village, which has shops and public toilets.

At the far end of the village, turn right and at the road end go right again, then left down to the riverbank. Follow the riverside path, again with several ups and downs over steps, to reach the footbridge at Dryburgh. Turn right over the bridge only if you wish to visit Dryburgh Abbey and the Wallace Statue.

Otherwise, climb the steps leading to a lovely viewpoint looking up the Tweed to the Eildon Hills. Follow the path along behind the Tweed Horizons Centre, then down three separate flights of steps to turn left and walk up a glen and go underneath the massive bridge carrying the A68, to reach Newtown St Boswells.

Shops and toilets are a short diversion to the right. The route goes straight across the junction, down a small road and straight across at the next crossroads to join the road to Whitelee. Pass under an old railway bridge and continue with the road for a kilometre.

When the road bends sharp left, go straight ahead through gates onto a clear path beside a fence. There may be horses here. After about 800m, go through another gate, then turn right downhill, through another gate and

Melrose from the Eildons.

across the bridge over the Bowden Burn. Turn left to follow the path beside the burn.

Go straight ahead at cross tracks, and when a road is reached, turn right into the village or left if you wish to visit Bowden Kirk. In the village, turn right and then first left and through a gate onto Bowden Common with the Eildons clear ahead.

Cross the common, go through a gate and into a plantation. Go down steps, leave the plantation and cross a field to go through gates across a red track and into the woods. Turn right and walk along the bottom of the wood to its far end. Turn left as signed and follow the signs up through the wood to a broad track higher up. Continue straight ahead along this track and follow it as it curves round to the left after about 800m, climbing to leave the wood at a gate.

Continue ahead to the col between the Eildon Hills, either or both of which can easily be climbed from here. At a fork, go right then immediately left on a small path, climbing a little to gain the col proper and your first view of Melrose and its Abbey. Follow the signs to walk down the main path, which slants down the hill.

At a fence, go through the wicket gate and continue down the fields through gates to reach a long flight of steps. At the foot of the steps go left across a footbridge and up to the road. Turn right and walk down Dingleton Road into Melrose, and journey's end.

Cargie's
Plantation
Borewell
Fm
LC
Scremerston
72
Inlandpasture
Woodside
Cott · 67
62·
Scremerston
Town Fm
B 6525
MP
PH
29
East Ho
Cheswick Ho
Ladythorne
Ho
Cheswick
Buildings
MP
East
Ancroft
26·
Broomhouse
Fm · 16
· 28
Ancroft Mill
Berryburn
Bridge Mill 12
New
Haggerston
38·
Berrington
51·
ROMAN ROAD

Saltpan Rocks
Cocklawburn Beach
Near Skerrs
Middle Skerr
Far Skerr
Cheswick Black
Rocks
Dunes
11· Cheswick
Shiel
Cheswick
Sands
Dunes
Cheswick
Dowie
Ho
LC
CH
17·
Windmill
Hill
· 12
North Low
Goswick
· 3
Haggerston
12
Castle
PC
19 Dovecote
23·
Brock Mill
Fm
The Mead
Haggerston
Barns
South Low
LC
4·
Beachcomber
Northumberland
Coast Path
Sluice
4
14· Beal
Point
8
A1
MP
4
LC
V 22
Beal
4
11
Go

© Crown Copyright. All rights reserved. Licence no. 100041103.

THE ISLANDSHIRE WAY: THE BERWICK LINK

The historic district of Islandshire mentioned earlier (see pages 68-9) at one time extended to the south bank of the Tweed at Tweedmouth. This walk therefore passes through both current and former areas of Islandshire.

SUMMARY

Distance: 17km (10.5 miles).

Height Range: Sea level to 30m.

Accommodation: Campsite at Goswick, hotels and B&Bs in Spittal, Tweedmouth and Berwick.

Food and Drink: Café at Borewell Farm (1km off route from Scremerston Sea House), pubs, cafés and restaurants in Spittal, Tweedmouth and Berwick.

Public Transport: Regular buses along the A1 at Beal, West Mains (5km from Causeway). Town bus service at Spittal. Buses and mainline railway station at Berwick.

Terrain Summary: A level coastal walk which can be wet initially. Dune and cliff scenery ending with a riverside walk into Berwick.

BEAL CAUSEWAY TO BERWICK RAILWAY STATION

From the Beal Causeway Car Park, join the northern-most stretch of the Northumberland Coast Path with its distinctive North Sea Trail logo. Walk alongside the concrete 'tank traps' and then follow the clear path along the foreshore to the low cliff of Beal Point and the mouth of the South Low. The path continues below the cliffs, and this next section can be inundated at high tide and is therefore often muddy. (There is an alternative route – from the causeway, follow the cycle path towards Beal then turn right along the cycle path to rejoin the trail at Longbridge Ends.)

Shortly after rounding the Point you will see a World War II 'pillbox' built into the cliff. The path keeps along the riverside until the sluice gate at Longbridge Ends is seen. Climb up the steps onto the flood bank ahead of you, turn right and follow the path over the sluice gate. Continue along the flood bank until you reach the edge of Goswick Dunes. The track curves round to the left. After 1.5km you reach a gate just beyond a path leading through the dunes onto Goswick Beach. In suitable tide conditions it is possible to take this path and walk along the beaches of Goswick, Cheswick and Cocklawburn and then rejoin the coastal path rather than continuing along the main track as described below.

Go through the gate and continue along the track towards Beachcomber House and the former Lookout Tower. (This was in use when Goswick Sands were used as a bombing range during World War II, and un-exploded bombs are still occasionally found in the area between Goswick beach and Holy Island.) Go through two further gates to join a metalled road which skirts the Beachcomber House camping and caravan site and then continues, past Goswick Farm on the left, to the Cheswick Golf Course Clubhouse. Follow the road, which turns left after the clubhouse, towards the level crossing where the Coastal Path fingerpost can be seen on the right-hand side just before the crossing.

Follow the clear track alongside the golf course, with the railway to your left, to reach a wall, then turn sharp right and follow the wall to a wicket gate on your left. The path continues along a bank above the golf course to a gate. Continue ahead across the field with Cheswick Dunes, some of the highest on the Northumberland coast, to your right and go through a further gate onto a road. Cross the road and join the surfaced cycle track which is part of National Cycle Route 1 (the Coast and Castles Cycle Route). Follow this track to a gate and stile with a pond on the left beyond the gate. The pond was formerly a limestone quarry providing lime for the nearby lime kilns. Continue along the cycle track towards a prominent World War II gun emplacement. Pass through a gate and join the public road. (A path out of the small car park behind this bunker leads towards a lime kiln built into the cliff at the southern end of Cocklawburn Beach.)

Continue along the road or, if preferred, descend to the beach which can be walked to its northern end if conditions permit. At the end of the beach, the road climbs to a cattle grid with the buildings of Scremerston Sea House ahead. Leave the road when it bends left and continue ahead on a clear track – again shared with the cycle route.

An airy clifftop walk follows with your ultimate destination – Berwick – visible in the distance. Cresting a hill after some 600m, Spittal Beach is seen for the first time and the track then descends gradually towards this seaside suburb of Berwick. If you require the amenities available – pubs, shops and a bus service – remain on the track, which leads into Spittal's main street. Otherwise, descend by the path to the right, down to the promenade. Walk along the promenade to its end, passing The Pavilion where refreshments are available (a public toilet is situated at the rear). Continue ahead on the path across the

Berwick from Tweedmouth.

grass to Sandstell Point with its car park at the mouth of
the Tweed. Leave the car park by the road and follow
it to a crossroads, with Spittal's main street coming in
from the left. Turn right and walk along the pavement to
the Lifeboat Station. Continue along the riverside green,
with superb views of Berwick's three bridges and the
Elizabethan Walls, and then past the Tweed Dock into
Tweedmouth's main street with its pubs, shops and cafés
until you reach the Old Bridge (completed in 1626).

Cross the Tweed on this bridge. On reaching the north-
ern side, you can either go straight ahead up the steep
West Street to reach the town centre, or turn sharp left
along the riverside to join a footpath known as the New
Road which runs alongside the river, passing under the
Royal Tweed Bridge. Follow the New Road towards the
Royal Border Bridge (1847-50) which carries the East
Coast Main Line over the Tweed. Just before reaching this
bridge, some steps on the right lead up to Castle Vale Park
and the railway station. Alternatively, you can continue
under the Royal Border Bridge and past the Water Tower
and the White Wall of Berwick's ruined castle with its
Breakyneck Steps going up the hill to the right. Continue
ahead on the path for a short distance until you come to
a gate on the right. This leads to a path which climbs up
the bank, with the castle walls to the right, and emerges
by the road bridge above Berwick station.

OTHER LINKING TRAILS

St Cuthbert's Way now links with a number of national and regional trails. As previously mentioned, European Long-Distance Footpath E2 follows part of St Cuthbert's Way to link the Southern Upland Way with the Pennine Way, but other trail combinations can be made. A list of these trails follows.

The Southern Upland Way, one of Scotland's four National Trails and Britain's first coast-to-coast trail, links Portpatrick on the Irish Sea with Cockburnspath on the North Sea, a distance of 340km (212 miles). It passes through Melrose.

www.dumgal.gov.uk/southernuplandway

Borders Abbeys Way. This 109km (68-mile) circular trail links the medieval Border Abbeys of Melrose, Dryburgh, Kelso and Jedburgh. It keeps company with St Cuthbert's Way for 800 metres from Jedfoot Bridge along Dere Street and also for a short stretch along the Tweed near Dryburgh footbridge.

www.scotborders.gov.uk/bordersabbeysway

The Pennine Way, Britain's first national trail, opened in 1965, links Edale in Derbyshire with Kirk Yetholm, a distance of 430km (270 miles). Its first 3km from Kirk Yetholm also form part of St Cuthbert's Way, after which it continues south following the Border Ridge to Byrness on the longest and most strenuous stage of its entire length.

www.nationaltrail.co.uk/PennineWay

The 8 km (5 mile) stretch of St Cuthbert's Way between the start of the Holy Island Causeway and Fawcet Hill has, since 2006, been shared with two new long-distance trails – the Northumberland Coast Path and St Oswald's Way.

Northumberland Coast Path. This 103km (64-mile) trail starts at Cresswell at the southern end of Druridge Bay and follows the coast as closely as possible to Berwick-upon-

Tweed. (The section from the Holy Island Causeway to
Berwick forms the Berwick Link described previously).
The path forms part of the North Sea Trail, a European
initiative that offers over 5,000km of the finest coastal
walking around the North Sea basin.

www.northumberlandcoastaonb.org
www.northseatrail.org

St Oswald's Way. This 156km (97-mile) trail links places
associated with the story of St Oswald, the early 7th
Century Northumbrian king. Starting at Holy Island, it
follows the Northumberland coast to the mouth of the
River Coquet and continues up the river to Rothbury. It
then crosses the Simonside Hills and the Harwood Forest before joining the Hadrian's Wall National Trail to
Heavenfield.

www.stoswaldsway.com

At Berwick-upon-Tweed the Northumberland Coast
Path links with the **Berwickshire Coastal Path** which
at present covers 24km (15 miles) as far as St Abbs. It is
hoped that eventually this path will reach Cockburnspath, thus linking up with the Southern Upland Way
and also the John Muir Way which continues round the
East Lothian coast.

INDEX

SOUVENIR CERTIFICATE

If you have completed St Cuthbert's Way as a continuous walk, you are invited to send for a St Cuthbert's Way Certificate by sending this form, duly certified at the points listed below, together with payment of £2 per certificate, to:

Countryside Access Team, Scottish Borders Council
Newtown St Boswells, Melrose, TD6 0SA

If certification points were closed when you did the walk, please enclose accommodation receipts or other proof of completion.

CERTIFICATION POINT	OFFICIAL STAMP OR SIGNATURE	DATE OF VISIT
Harestanes Countryside Visitor Centre, by Ancrum, Jedburgh (open April-October)		
Tourist Information Centre, Cheviot Centre Padgepool Place, Wooler (open April-October)		
Post Office, Marygate, Holy Island		

Name ....

Address ....

.... Postcode ....

Name(s) to appear on Certificate(s) ....

....

Number of people in your party ....

IT WOULD BE VERY HELPFUL IF YOU WOULD KINDLY COMPLETE THE QUESTIONNAIRE OVERLEAF

ST CUTHBERT'S WAY QUESTIONNAIRE

Please tick to show the type of accommodation you used while walking the Way

(Tick more than one box if appropriate)

HOTEL ☐   **BED & BREAKFAST** ☐

YOUTH HOSTEL ☐   **CAMPING** ☐

OTHER (please specify)...

How many days did you take to walk the Trail?

What was your average daily spend?

£0–£20 ☐   £21–£50 ☐   £50 or over ☐

We would be grateful for your assessment of various facilities connected with St Cuthbert's Way (please tick as appropriate)

	POOR	ADEQUATE	GOOD	VERY GOOD
The Trail Guide	☐	☐	☐	☐
Waymarking	☐	☐	☐	☐
Condition of Trail	☐	☐	☐	☐

Please use the space below to report any difficulties encountered along St Cuthbert's Way (please give as much detail as possible, including grid references if possible)